the healthy

COCONUT FLOUR COOKBOOK

>=<

MORE THAN **100**
♥ GRAIN-FREE ♥ GLUTEN-FREE
♥ PALEO-FRIENDLY
RECIPES FOR EVERY OCCASION

♥ ♥ ♥

ERICA KERWIEN

FAIR WINDS

Brimming with creative inspiration, how-to projects, and useful information to enrich your everyday life, Quarto Knows is a favorite destination for those pursuing their interests and passions. Visit our site and dig deeper with our books into your area of interest: Quarto Creates, Quarto Cooks, Quarto Homes, Quarto Lives, Quarto Drives, Quarto Explores, Quarto Gifts, or Quarto Kids.

©2014 Fair Winds Press
Text and photography ©2014 Erica Kerwien

First published in 2014 by Fair Winds Press,
an imprint of The Quarto Group,
100 Cummings Center, Suite 265-D,
Beverly, MA 01915, USA.
T (978) 282-9590 F (978) 283-2742
www.QuartoKnows.com

All rights reserved. No part of this book may be reproduced in any form without written permission of the copyright owners. All images in this book have been reproduced with the knowledge and prior consent of the artists concerned, and no responsibility is accepted by producer, publisher, or printer for any infringement of copyright or otherwise, arising from the contents of this publication. Every effort has been made to ensure that credits accurately comply with information supplied. We apologize for any inaccuracies that may have occurred and will resolve inaccurate or missing information in a subsequent reprinting of the book.

Fair Winds Press titles are also available at discount for retail, wholesale, promotional, and bulk purchase. For details, contact the Special Sales Manager by email at specialsales@quarto.com or by mail at The Quarto Group, Attn: Special Sales Manager, 401 Second Avenue North, Suite 310, Minneapolis, MN 55401, USA.

18 17   7 8 9 10

ISBN: 978-1-59233-546-6
Digital edition published in 2014
eISBN: 978-1-62788-011-4

Library of Congress Cataloging-in-Publication Data available

Cover and Book design by Debbie Berne Design
Book layout by Sporto
Photography by Erica Kerwien

Printed and bound in China

The information in this book is for educational purposes only. It is not intended to replace the advice of a physician or medical practitioner. Please see your health care provider before beginning any new health program.

To my family and friends,
and to my extended family of recipe testers
and Comfy Belly readers

Contents

CHAPTER 1

THE WONDERS OF COCONUT FLOUR

When it comes to coconut flour, there's so much to love. High in fiber
and protein, low in carbohydrates, gluten-free—it's no wonder so many
following gluten-free and grain-free diets are singing its praises!

But what *is* coconut flour, you might ask? Simply put, it's the finely ground,
fiber-rich dried coconut that remains after coconut oil is extracted from coconut
flesh. A pure, natural, one-ingredient product, it's a healthy alternative to wheat
and other gluten-free flours and works well in a wide variety of recipes that call
for flour. It's also higher in protein than most gluten-free flours—including oat
bran and ground flaxseed—and has about the same protein content as buckwheat
and whole wheat flours, making it nutrient-rich while also being wheat-free.

Whether it's your first or fortieth time using coconut flour, you
are in for a real treat. Read on to learn more about the flour and
the best methods for getting delicious, healthy results.

Where Can I Find Coconut Flour?

You can purchase coconut flour in most well-stocked grocery stores or online. The two brands I recommend—and used for the creation of this book—are Honeyville Farms and Tropical Traditions (both organic), though there are several other reliable sources that you can look into (see page 154). Keep in mind that not all coconut flour has the same finely ground texture, which may affect how a recipe turns out.

I don't make my own coconut flour because it's easier and more affordable for me to buy great quality, finely ground, organic versions online; however, if you want to or need to make it, you can. Use dried, unsweetened, shredded coconut or coconut flakes and grind in a spice or coffee grinder until it is as fine as possible, with the goal being to get the flour to a powderlike consistency. Just a warning: Your results may vary so your best bet is to use commercially prepared coconut flour (see Resources, page 154).

The Many Health Benefits of Coconut Flour

Coconut flour offers an array of health benefits. Two of my favorites being that it is naturally high in fiber and low in carbohydrates.

BETTER FOR BLOOD SUGAR

Blood sugar (also referred to as blood glucose) is the amount of glucose in our blood, which we rely on for energy. Blood sugar increases after we eat, and our bodies respond to the increase by releasing a hormone called *insulin* to control the level of sugar in our blood so that it doesn't get too high. A rapid drop in blood sugar, on the other hand, is controlled by a hormone called *glucagen*, which stimulates the release of more sugar in our blood. This balancing of blood sugar is at play all the time and especially after we eat.

Because the carbohydrates we eat are broken down into glucose they have a greater effect on our blood sugar. Food and meals that are high in carbohydrates, for example, can cause a rapid rise in blood sugar, which forces our bodies to respond. This sudden rise stresses the body as the pancreas pumps a large amount of insulin to manage the rush of blood sugar. Over time, high blood sugar levels can lead to or complicate various health issues, including diabetes, weight gain, heart disease, hypoglycemia, and overall health.

Fortunately, coconut flour helps to keep our blood sugar at a healthy level thanks to its high fiber content. How, you might ask? Well, the fiber in coconut flour is low in digestible carbohydrates so it doesn't have the same effect on our blood sugar compared to other carbohydrates such as wheat grains and rice. To give you an idea of how high in fiber it is, coconut flour has four times the amount of fiber as oat bran and two times that of wheat bran! As this fiber goes through our digestive systems, it helps digest food, makes us feel full, and cleans out other residue before leaving our bodies.

STAYING HYDRATED

Coconut flour's naturally high fiber content means that it sweeps through your digestive system, brushing away indigestible residue and debris. It also absorbs moisture along the way, so you'll want to make sure you're taking in enough fluids to balance it all out! A nice cup of tea, milk, or whatever you fancy always goes great with coconut flour treats.

HEALTHY WEIGHT MAINTENANCE

Since coconut flour is high in indigestible fiber, it gives you the feeling of being full without all the added calories from digestible carbohydrates. A little coconut flour muffin, for instance, may fill you up much more than its refined, store-bought counterpart, all of which helps in maintaining portion control and a healthy weight.

In addition, coconut flour is slightly sweet on its own so you can usually reduce the amount of sweetener used in recipes made with it, which means fewer calories without sacrificing taste.

GRAIN- AND GLUTEN-FREE

Coconut flour works well for gluten-free and allergy-free lifestyles since it's naturally gluten-free and isn't a common food allergen (coconut is actually a fruit and not a nut, despite the name). Several grains and gluten-free grains, such as wheat and corn, are much higher on the potential allergy or intolerance scale. (To figure out if you may have a food intolerance, eliminate it from your diet for a week or so to see if your symptoms improve.)

Coconut flour is an amazingly versatile gluten-free flour as it can be used on its own, or in combination with other flours. Using coconut flour on its own can be a huge bonus if you need to avoid other types of flour, or want or need to reduce your consumption of nuts and nut flour (which are calorie dense).

Coconut flour also has the effect of yielding lighter baked goods because it is not as heavy as nut flours and a little bit of it goes a much longer way, with great-tasting results. Most of the recipes in this book are made only with coconut flour, while others incorporate a small to moderate amount of nut flour for a complementary effect, as I'll discuss below.

STORING YOUR COCONUT FLOUR

Coconut flour tends to absorb moisture so it's a good idea to keep it well sealed. If you're not using it within a few weeks, I suggest storing it in the refrigerator and bringing it to room temperature before using in a recipe.

Making Things Sweet

I'm partial to using the natural sweeteners you'll see in this book as most are raw or minimally processed so that they retain

nutrients and vitamins beneficial to your health. While you may not always be able to find an organic source for a sweetener, choosing unrefined sweeteners that don't have additives and are sustainably produced will be healthier for your body and the environment.

HONEY

The various flavors, colors, and viscosities of honey depend on the flowers the bees are pollinating and the region in which the honey is collected, sometimes referred to as the honey's *terroir*. I generally bake with clover honey that is local to my region. Occasionally a darker honey, such as buckwheat or blackberry, works well in a recipe when you want to emulate the flavor of molasses.

Ideally you'll want to buy your honey raw, unfiltered, and unprocessed; however, pasteurized honey works well, too. It's good to know where your honey comes from since there've been several incidents of poor quality "sugared-down" honey on market shelves in the last few years.

Store honey in sealed containers at room temperature. If the honey crystallizes, place the container in a warm bowl of water for a few minutes to make it runny again. To measure, rub a little drop of oil in the measuring cup or spoon, and then fill it with the desired amount of honey, so it slides out easily.

MAPLE SYRUP

Maple syrup is one of my favorite sweeteners because I like the flavor it gives baked goods and it has a higher concentration of minerals than honey. Maple syrup is a great source of manganese and zinc, important to your immune system function.

Real maple syrup, from the light to the very dark and in between, has an earthy, sweet flavor. Maple syrup is categorized as either Grade A or Grade B. Grade A tends to be lighter and has a mellow flavor while Grade B is darker and has a deeper, earthier flavor. Both grades work in my recipes; just note that you may have a more pronounced maple flavor if you're using Grade B.

DATES

Dates are the fruit from the date palm tree. They are naturally sweet and best used when soft. Store in the refrigerator until use (they should last several months) and bring to room temperature before using in a recipe.

For some recipes—or if your dates are old or very dry—you may need to soften

IS YOUR HONEY TOO THICK?

∽∾

Some raw honey is thicker than others, which depends on many effects, including time of year, where the bees were harvesting the nectar, and what kind of flowers and plants they were visiting. If your honey is too thick to measure, place the container in a warm bowl of water for a few minutes to make it a bit more pourable.

them in warm water for an hour or so before draining and pitting. Process them separately or along with the other ingredients in a food processor before adding them to the recipe.

COCONUT SUGAR

Coconut sugar, also known as coconut palm sugar, is made from the flowers of the coconut palm, found mainly in South and Southeast Asia. You may also have heard of palm sugar or date sugar, which is different than coconut sugar and is made from date palm.

Coconut sugar is brown in color with a subtly sweet caramel flavor. It has a lower glycemic index than most sweeteners, making it a popular sweetener for diabetics or anyone trying to lower their blood sugar. It is a bit less sweet than commercial granulated sugar (white and brown), but can be used as a 1:1 substitute for either of these in recipes.

STEVIA

Stevia is a natural sweetener derived from the leaves of the *Stevia rebaudiana* plant. It has no calories or carbohydrates and zero glycemic index so it's often used to reduce or replace sugar in recipes. That said, it's about ten to fifteen times sweeter than other natural sweeteners so it doesn't take much stevia to sweeten a recipe. It can also have a slightly bitter aftertaste depending on how it's used and it doesn't caramelize like other sweeteners, so it works best in small amounts and in recipes where there are other sources of sweetness, such as honey, maple syrup, or fruit. The sweetness also varies by brand.

WHAT IS MAPLE SUGAR?

Maple sugar is made by evaporating all the water from maple syrup. It has a similar taste and consistency to brown sugar but is more expensive than brown sugar or coconut sugar. While it can be used as a brown sugar replacement, I use it in small quantities as an accent or an accompaniment to other sweeteners. For instance, it works well in the Snickerdoodles cinnamon topping recipe (page 109).

While there's no steadfast ratio for replacing sugar with stevia (as strength varies based on brand and whether it's powder or liquid), a general ratio for replacing liquid sweeteners such as maple syrup is to use ½ teaspoon of powdered stevia plus ¼ cup (60 ml) of a liquid to replace ¼ cup (80 g) maple syrup. The added liquid makes up for the loss of liquid from the maple syrup; I usually use coconut milk or water, but you can use any kind of milk or other liquid you like.

Complementary Flours

There are a number of gluten-free flours that can complement coconut flour in a recipe, and I use a few of them in this book, especially for the grain-free recipes. Here is a bit more about them.

ALMOND FLOUR

Almond flour, or blanched almond flour, is finely ground, raw, blanched almonds. It is

ALMOND FLOUR VS. ALMOND MEAL

∽✦∽

Not to be confused with blanched almond flour, almond meal is ground up almonds with the skins left on instead of blanched off. Almond meal works well in hardier or more rustic recipes and has a slightly more grainy texture because of the skins.

higher in protein and good fats than most flours and tastes great in baked goods such as cookies, cakes, muffins, and pie crusts.

You can make it at home by first blanching (soaking and peeling the skins off of) raw almonds and then grinding the dried almonds in a food processor. Another trick is to buy blanched whole almonds (or slivers or pieces) and process them in a food processor or high-speed blender until you have a fine flour.

I much prefer buying finely ground blanched almond flour because it is invariably more fine and uniform in texture than what I can produce at home. I use Honeyville's blanched almond flour, but there are many reliable sources to choose from. See Resources, (page 154), for the brands I recommend.

PUMPKIN SEED AND OTHER SEED FLOURS

Some recipes in this book combine almond flour with coconut flour. However, if you can't or don't eat almonds, you'll mostly likely be able to replace it with a seed flour such as finely ground pumpkin seeds or sunflower

seeds. The flavor and consistency of the result may vary a bit depending on the seed you use. To make seed flour, grind the seeds in a spice grinder, coffee bean grinder, or dry blender until it is the consistency of flour.

CASHEW FLOUR

Cashew flour is most often made from raw cashews as opposed to roasted cashews. You can make it yourself by grinding up raw cashews in a food processor or high-speed blender with a dry blade (such as a Vitamix) to make a fine flour. If you're just trying to replace almond flour with another nut flour, cashew flour is a good substitute for most recipes, especially muffins, cakes, and cookies.

HAZELNUT FLOUR

Hazelnut flour is made from ground up roasted hazelnuts and is easy to make at home (and usually less expensive). The nuts must

HOW TO REMOVE THE SKINS FROM HAZELNUTS

∽✦∽

To remove the skins from hazelnuts (also referred to as filberts), preheat your oven to 300°F (150°C, or gas mark 2). Spread the hazelnuts in a single layer across a rimmed baking sheet and toast for 10 minutes. Remove the hazelnuts from the oven and cool. Place the nuts in a towel and rub to remove as much of the skins as possible. Don't worry if you can't get all of the skins off; what comes off easily is enough.

first be roasted and cooled, then de-skinned and ground. Store any excess flour in the freezer as nut flours tend to go rancid more quickly than other flours.

PECAN FLOUR

Pecan flour is ground up roasted raw or roasted pecans. It goes well in recipes for hardy muffins, sweet breads, pancakes, and waffles. To make it at home, place toasted and cooled pecans in a food processor or dry high-speed blender container and pulse until the pecans become a fine flour. Store any excess flour in the refrigerator or freezer.

Good Oils and Fats

Oils are obtained by pressing oil-rich plants enough to release their oils. Oils that I like to use and that you'll see in this book include olive oil, nut and seed oils, and coconut oil. I try to stick with those that are minimally processed, so I look for words like "cold-pressed" and "unrefined." I do also use refined oils on occasion, but only for high-heat cooking and only from trusted brands and sources, such as Spectrum Organics. Aside from the dairy-free oils mentioned above, I also use butter and ghee, organic and from grass-fed animals whenever possible.

I don't mind spending a little extra money on healthy fats and oils that are minimally processed and from reliable sources because the fats they contain are essential to good health and help our bodies absorb and process fat-soluble minerals and vitamins.

WHAT IS PALM SHORTENING?

Palm shortening is made with palm oil and is a nonhydrogenated alternative to traditional shortening. The nice thing about palm shortening—aside from containing no trans fats—is that it doesn't impart any flavor or aroma to a recipe, can be used at high heat, and has a long shelf-life. See Resources, page 154, to find out brands and sources.

If you can't find palm shortening, coconut oil and vegetable shortening can be used interchangeably, as they both have a high smoke point and are good for baking and cooking at high temperatures (and are dairy-free), but keep in mind that coconut oil may impart more of a flavor—which may or may not be desirable.

While I use both dairy-based and dairy-free fats in my cooking, you can easily bake and cook dairy-free using just coconut oil and other plant-based oils and fats.

That said, it is important to keep in mind the smoke point of various oils when cooking and baking. For high-heat applications, I avoid using oils that smoke or burn at a lower temperature, such as olive oil, butter, and many unrefined oils. The oils that can be used at cooking and baking temperatures above 350°F (180°C, or gas mark 4) include refined coconut oil, ghee, high-heat cooking oil, and palm shortening. Look at your labels (they should say) if you're unsure of your oil's smoke point and be sure to stay under that mark when heating.

Milks and Creams

There's a variety of creams and milks that can be used in the recipes in this book. Some are dairy based and some are dairy-free. Many of the dairy-free milks such as coconut, hazelnut, almond, and rice milk are subtly sweet, making them a nice substitute for dairy-based milks such as cow and goat milk.

My favorite dairy-free milks are almond and coconut milk; however, it is challenging to find commercial versions of dairy-free milks without additives. The nice thing is it's fairly easy to make them from scratch; you just need to have some raw almonds or unsweetened shredded coconut on hand. I make almond milk from scratch and sometimes I make coconut milk from scratch. When it comes to store-bought dairy-free milks, look for those that have few or no additives and come in BPA-free or nontoxic packaging.

If you have no need to avoid dairy, feel free to use regular milk in any recipe that calls for dairy-free milk such as coconut milk, unless noted otherwise. Likewise, if you do need to avoid dairy, sub in dairy-free milk, unless noted otherwise. For whipped cream, you can easily make Coconut Whipped Cream (page 100).

Homemade Coconut Milk

Since I've found a brand of coconut milk that contains no additives (AROY-D), I don't make it from scratch often, but I do find it convenient to whip up when I'm out of store-bought or just need a little bit of milk and don't want to open a new container or can. You can make this in a matter of minutes if you're rushed for time, whereas almond milk requires about 8 hours of soaking time.

1 cup (64 g) unsweetened shredded coconut (see Resources, page 154)

2 cups (475 ml) water

1. Combine the coconut and water in a blender container and let soak for about 2 hours. Or, if you're short on time, soak the coconut in hot water (about the temperature of hot tap water) for a few minutes and move on to the next step.
2. Blend in a high-speed blender on the highest speed for a minute or two.
3. Strain the coconut milk through several layers of cheesecloth or a nut milk bag into a pitcher or bowl; discard solids. Store the milk in the refrigerator. It will last for several days.

Yield: 2 cups (475 ml)

Homemade Almond Milk

Almond milk is a naturally sweet, dairy-free milk that can be used in place of any other milk in most of the recipes in this book. All you need are almonds, water, and a bit of preplanning. And be sure to give the soaked almonds a try on their own; they make a great, filling snack, and they're easy to digest this way!

1 cup (145 g) raw almonds

2 cups (475 ml) water

1. Place the almonds in a bowl and cover them with the water. Soak overnight or at least 8 to 10 hours.

2. Drain and rinse the almonds and place them in a high-speed blender. Add the water and blend until almonds are completely ground up; I blend mine for about 1 minute.

3. Strain the almond milk through a nut milk bag or several layers of cheesecloth into a pitcher or bowl; discard solids. Store the milk in the refrigerator. It will last for several days.

Yield: 2 cups (475 ml)

Substituting Ingredients in a Recipe

Substituting ingredients successfully can vary from recipe to recipe. You'll want to take into account how swapping out one ingredient for another will affect the overall taste and texture of a dish. Some recipes in this book are flexible enough that you can substitute one ingredient for another, such as nondairy milk for regular milk, as mentioned above. I've made a note in those recipes where substitutions were tested and are possible. If there are other substitutions you are keen on making, read through the following tips and techniques—and note that results may vary!

REPLACING EGGS

The egg is a tricky ingredient to swap out because it is a flavorless and, often vital, binding agent used quite generously in most coconut flour recipes. Eggs can be replicated *somewhat* with the following alternatives.

DUCK EGGS FOR SENSITIVITY

If you're having a problem digesting chicken eggs, sometimes you can replace them with duck eggs to see if that relieves you of any intolerance. Just keep an eye on size so you're not substituting in more (or less) egg, as duck eggs are larger than chicken eggs.

Puréed Fruit

Bananas and applesauce not only act as binding agents and add sweetness, but either can also be used as a substitute for oil or butter (though I wouldn't substitute both the eggs and fat in the same recipe). Keep in mind, however, that banana has a distinct flavor, so use it when you want that flavor. Puréed prunes (baby food) also bind and add sweetness. These replacements work best in baked goods that are small in size, such as in cookies, muffins, and cupcakes.

¼ cup (56 g) mashed banana = 1 egg

¼ cup (60 g) unsweetened applesauce = 1 egg

3 tablespoons puréed prunes (45 g) = 1 egg

Yogurt (Dairy-Based or Dairy-Free)

Yogurt can also be used to replace eggs and adds moisture to batter. If you're dairy-free, use a dairy-free yogurt such as coconut, almond, or rice. Like banana and applesauce, yogurt works well in baked goods that are small in size.

¼ cup (60 g) yogurt = 1 egg

Flaxseed Meal

Flaxseed meal is ground flaxseeds and can be used as a moist binding agent. I've tested it well in the Chocolate Chip Cookies (page 107), and it will work with other muffin, cupcake, and cookie recipes in this book. I keep a small amount of flaxseeds in my refrigerator and place them in a coffee or spice grinder to grind them into meal as needed, as fresh is best.

1 tablespoon (7 g) of flaxseed meal + 3 tablespoons (45 ml) of water = 1 egg

Baking Soda

Baking soda plus vinegar can also be used to replace eggs, although I've found this technique to be less reliable than the other substitutes, so proceed with caution. Add the baking soda to the dry ingredients in the recipe and add the vinegar to the wet ingredients, then combine the dry and wet ingredients. A chemical reaction will release gas and lift your batter. Place the batter in the oven as soon as you combine the dry and wet ingredients, before the gas can escape.

1 teaspoon (4.6 g) baking soda + 1 teaspoon (5 ml) apple cider vinegar = 1 egg

REPLACING SWEETENERS

Sweeteners can often be substituted for one another in recipes, depending on preference. Dates are an excellent alternative to honey or maple syrup (my favorite date is the Medjool but others work, too), just be sure they are nice and moist. I often find it best to soak them in hot water, then drain, pit, and process them in a food processor until they are similar in consistency to what the honey or maple syrup would have provided and blend well into cake and bread batters.

¼ cup (85 g) honey or maple syrup = ¼ cup (45 g) chopped dates, blended

1 tablespoon honey (20 g) or maple syrup = 2 pitted dates, blended

When I talked about stevia earlier, a general ratio was given for replacing liquid sweeteners like maple syrup or honey with stevia (**½ teaspoon of powdered stevia + ¼ cup (60 ml) of a liquid = ¼ cup (80 g) maple syrup**). The liquid makes up for the loss of liquid from the maple syrup—I usually use coconut milk or water, but you can use any kind of milk you like.

Baking Tips

There are a few things about coconut flour and baking in general that are good to know before you get started. As coconut flour behaves much differently than many other flours, knowing its "personality" is imperative for baking success!

A LITTLE COCONUT FLOUR GOES A LONG WAY

Coconut flour will go a long way in baking which means you don't need much—often ¼ to ½ cup (26 to 52 g)—to bake an entire bread or cake. While most recipes using coconut flour require less flour, they do require more moisture, or liquid, than traditional and gluten-free flours because of the high fiber content.

WATCH THE MOISTURE FACTOR

Coconut flour acts as a hydrocolloid when placed in a moist batter, absorbing moisture and binding ingredients together, so it's great to use with wet ingredients. Keep in mind

that coconut flour takes a few minutes or so to absorb this moisture, so let a batter sit for a few minutes before baking or going on to the next step. I usually let a batter sit for 5 minutes after incorporating the flour, mix or blend once more, and then go on.

If your flour is clumpy upon measuring, you can first whisk or sift it either on its own or with the other dry ingredients. It doesn't take much effort to sift the flour, so I usually just mix it up a bit in my stand mixer or whisk it for a moment to break up any clumps before adding it to the wet ingredients.

MEASURE FLOUR CAREFULLY

Weighing flour (in grams) for a recipe is the most accurate way to measure it. That said, I have included measurements for flour and

CONVERTING RECIPES ON YOUR OWN: BAKER BEWARE

You may be tempted to take your favorite recipes and replace the type of flour called for with coconut flour, but it's rarely going to be a 1:1 substitution unless you make various adjustments to other ingredients, and the result is likely to be much different (often for the worse), so it's not something I'd recommend. Stick to the recipes in this book and you'll be much better off!

other dry ingredients in both grams and cups in this book, so either will work. I don't pack flour when measuring, but instead use the spoon-and-swipe method, lightly scooping flour into the measuring cup, then using a knife or other edge to level it off the top so it's fairly even.

If you're looking for the very best result, weighing your flour is the way to go every time. For coconut flour, all the weights are based on Honeyville's organic coconut flour. Other brands will either weigh the same or come close, but be aware that the textures may vary. Brands that I've found have about the same weight and consistency as Honeyville are listed in the Resources section (page 154).

MAKE EGGS YOUR FRIEND

Eggs are an essential part of coconut flour recipes as they act as both a binding and moisture agent. While you may be able to substitute a few of the eggs with applesauce, banana, or other egg substitutes, it will depend on the recipe and other ingredients, and may require some experimenting. (You can use flaxseed meal as an egg substitute in the Chocolate Chip Cookies on page 107 without a problem, as I've tested and noted.)

All of the recipes in this book use large eggs. In general, when a recipe calls for "1 egg" and doesn't specify a size, use a large egg. Based on the United States Department of Agriculture sizing chart:

1 large egg = 2 ounces = 57 g = 46 ml = 3¼ tablespoons

Not all egg sizes are created equal due to varying standards across countries, so make sure your eggs are in this range or close to it, or adjust the number of eggs up or down depending on their size or weight. Canadian eggs tend to be a bit larger than U.S. eggs, while European eggs are a whole size larger.

Helpful Kitchen Tools and Materials

Below are some kitchen tools and materials that you'll find quite helpful, or possibly indispensable, and ones that I highly recommend you have for the recipes in this book. Some of them, such as a food processor and stand mixer, can do double or even triple duty and are well worth the investment if you cook or bake a lot. A food processor, for example, can be used to blend a cake batter, grind nuts into nut flour, and purée a soup or smoothie!

My favorite tools include:

- Whisks and spatulas
- Measuring spoons, cups, and a digital kitchen scale
- Food processor
- Mixer (stand or handheld)
- High-speed blender (great for nut and seed butters, smoothies, soups, and even nut flours)

Aside from those listed previously, there are some tools that you'll need for only some of the recipes in this book, but they are fun and helpful to have on hand if you spend a lot of time in the kitchen. They include:

- Baking sheets and pans
- Bread and cake pans
- Cupcake or muffin pans (or silicon muffin cups)
- Box grater for shaving, grating, and shredding (or you can use the food processor attachment)
- Waffle iron
- Donut pan or donut maker

My favorite materials for baking are:

- Parchment paper
- Silpat nonstick baking mats
- Parchment paper cupcake or muffin liners (see Resources, page 154)

I rely quite a bit on parchment paper when baking with coconut flour, as some of the batters are quite sticky. I keep a roll of parchment paper and parchment paper cupcake or muffin liners on hand for all my baking needs. I also use Silpat nonstick baking mats—primarily with cookies, scones, and biscuits—to make post-baking cleanup easy.

To get a good fitting circle of parchment paper for the inside of a cake or bread pan, trace the pan on the parchment paper and then cut out the traced shape. I often grease

HOW TO MAKE PARCHMENT LINERS

Parchment liners for cupcakes and muffins are a fun way to make your baked goods even more enticing. To make liners, cut a large sheet of parchment paper into 5-inch (13 cm) squares. Lightly grease your muffin or cupcake pan and press a parchment square into each cup, folding and overlapping along the creases (see photo at left). Carefully pour the batter into each liner and bake as directed. Serve with liners on for a nice presentation and easy packaging.

the inside of the pan and then place the cut-out paper in the pan. Once the cake or bread is baked you can remove it more easily because the bottom won't stick! Or you can just leave the paper in until you're finished using the pan.

Let's Get Started!

Baking and cooking is a fun adventure with great rewards at the finish line. But before you dive in, just remember my final few tips: bring ingredients to room temperature before beginning, read the recipe at least once before starting, and don't be afraid to get messy. Eat well, be well!

CHAPTER 2

BREADS, BISCUITS, AND PIZZA

The smell of baking bread or the sight of a steaming basket of biscuits never gets old and is certainly one of the many perks of baking at home. In this chapter, coconut flour is combined with a medley of nutritious and flavorful ingredients—including fresh herbs, roasted vegetables, berries, zucchini, and even cauliflower—to create delicious breads and biscuits that everyone is sure to enjoy. And as a bonus, most recipes are quick and easy, so the payoff is a fast one! Others take a bit longer, but the reward is more than worth it.

Everyday Popovers

•Gluten-Free •Grain-Free •Dairy-Free •Low-Sugar •Paleo •Nut-Free

Popovers are the American variation of English Yorkshire Pudding. This recipe yields popovers that are just as you'd expect. They're light, almost hollow, and easy to make at a moment's notice. You can add a variety of ingredients depending on your taste; I've included both a savory and a sweet popover recipe following this basic one to give you some ideas. Just note that you'll want to bake the popovers in nonstick popover sleeves, parchment paper, or muffin liners. See page 23 on how to make your own liners.

4 large eggs

½ cup (120 ml) coconut milk or other milk

⅛ teaspoon salt

2 tablespoons (13 g) coconut flour

1. Preheat your oven to 425°F (220°C, or gas mark 7).

2. Add all the ingredients to a bowl and whisk until fully blended and a bit bubbly. The batter will have a liquid consistency.

3. Fill muffin liners or nonstick popover sleeves about two-thirds of the way with batter.

4. Bake for 15 minutes, or until they begin to brown on top, keeping the oven door closed to prevent them from collapsing.

5. Cool for a moment and serve. These are best served soon after they come out of the oven, but can be kept covered and warm for a while as well.

Yield: 6 popovers

Parmesan-Thyme Popovers

•Gluten-Free   •Grain-Free   •Low-Sugar   •Nut-Free

A combination of herbs and aged cheese makes for a light, savory roll that is the perfect accompaniment to any meal, soup, or stew. You can replace the Parmesan with another hard or soft cheese such as Pecorino or cheddar, or try adding pesto, garlic, chives, and other herbs to create your favorite mix.

4 large eggs

½ cup (120 ml) coconut milk or other milk

2 tablespoons (13 g) coconut flour

Pinch salt (less than ⅛ teaspoon)

1 tablespoon (5 g) grated Parmesan cheese

1 tablespoon (2.4 g) chopped fresh thyme

1. Preheat your oven to 425°F (220°C, or gas mark 7).

2. Add all the ingredients to a bowl and whisk until fully blended and a bit bubbly. The batter will have a liquid consistency.

3. Fill muffin liners or nonstick popover sleeves one-half to two-thirds of the way with batter.

4. Bake for about 15 minutes, or until they begin to brown on top, keeping the oven door closed to prevent them from collapsing.

5. Cool for a moment and serve. These are best served soon after they come out of the oven, but can be kept covered and warm for a while as well.

Yield: 6 popovers

Cinnamon Popovers

•Gluten-Free •Grain-Free •Dairy-Free •Low-Sugar •Paleo •Nut-Free

Adding a bit of cinnamon and sweetener creates a popover that is reminiscent of French toast. These are fair game for a dip in maple syrup when they're straight out of the oven, but feel free to eat them any way you like. They're great with fruit and jam as well. This recipe can take just about any kind of liquid or dry sweetener, and it doesn't need too much. Do watch them in the oven, though, because they tend to brown a bit faster with the added sweetener.

4 large eggs

½ cup (120 ml) coconut milk or other milk

2 teaspoons (13 g) honey or other sweetener

½ teaspoon ground cinnamon

2 tablespoons (13 g) coconut flour

Pinch salt (less than ⅛ teaspoon)

1. Preheat your oven to 425°F (220°C, or gas mark 7).

2. Add all the ingredients to a bowl and whisk until fully blended and a bit bubbly. The batter will have a liquid consistency.

3. Fill the muffin liners about two-thirds of the way with batter.

4. Bake for about 12 minutes, or until they start to brown on top, keeping the oven door closed to prevent them from collapsing.

5. Cool for a moment and serve. These are best served soon after they come out of the oven, but they can be kept covered and warm for a while as well.

Yield: 6 popovers

Cauliflower Pizza Crust

•Gluten-Free •Grain-Free •Low-Sugar •Nut-Free

Creating a pizza crust using cauliflower requires a few more steps than other grain-free, gluten-free pizza crusts, but the flavor and texture of this pizza is worth the extra effort. It's the kind of crust that's tender and thick, like a deep-dish or thick, doughy crust, thanks in part to the delicious cheese that accompanies the cauliflower.

To rice the cauliflower, use a box grater or food processor to grate the cauliflower florets into rice-size pieces without letting it get mushy.

2 cups (232 g) grated cauliflower florets (about 1 medium cauliflower head)

1 medium garlic clove, peeled and pressed or finely minced

¼ teaspoon salt

2 teaspoons (1.5 g) chopped fresh herbs (oregano, basil, rosemary, or other)

1 egg

2 tablespoons (13 g) coconut flour

½ cup (44 g) grated Parmesan cheese or other cheese, or a mix of grated hard and soft cheeses

1. Preheat your oven to 450°F (230°C, or gas mark 8).

2. Line baking sheets with parchment paper or other nonstick surface.

3. Place the cauliflower florets in a food processor and pulse until the florets are finely riced. Alternatively, you can grate the florets using a box or cheese grater.

4. Prepare a steamer and steam the riced cauliflower, about 5 minutes, or until it is just tender but not soft throughout.

5. Cool the rice and remove all excess moisture by placing it in a nut milk bag, cheesecloth, or dish towel and squeezing it over the sink. If the cauliflower is hot, wear dish-washing gloves when doing this step.

6. Add the cauliflower, garlic, salt, herbs, egg, coconut flour, and cheese to a mixing bowl and blend well.

7. On parchment paper or a nonstick surface, shape the mixture into two small circles, or one large circle or square, about ½-inch (1.3 cm) thick. The dough is fairly loose so use your hands to shape and flatten it.

8. Bake the pizza crust for about 10 minutes, or until the edges begin to brown. Now you can add toppings and bake for another 5 minutes, or you can store the crusts in a sealed container in the refrigerator for a few days or in the freezer for a few months.

Yield: 1 large or 2 small pizza crusts, or about 4 servings

REMOVING MOISTURE FROM THE CAULIFLOWER

The goal here is to get rid of as much moisture from the steamed cauliflower as possible. Place all the steamed cauliflower in a dish towel, nut milk bag, cheesecloth, or fine-mesh strainer and squeeze the cauliflower to release as much water as possible. Protect your hands by wearing dish-washing gloves if you're handling hot cauliflower.

Garlic-Cauliflower Breadsticks

•Gluten-Free   •Grain-Free   •Low-Sugar   •Nut-Free

When you're in the mood for pizza-style breadsticks with marinara sauce and cheese, but without the extra carbohydrates that come from grain-based crusts, you'll be happy you have this in your repertoire. Cauliflower lends itself well to yielding a thick, soft crust, be it in pizza or breadstick form—you'll be amazed that it's completely grain-free!

2 cups (232 g) grated cauliflower

½ cup (44 g) grated Parmesan cheese or other cheese, or a mix of hard and soft cheeses, divided

1 garlic clove, peeled and pressed or finely minced

¼ teaspoon salt

2 teaspoons (1.5 g) chopped fresh herbs (oregano, basil, rosemary, or other), or 1 teaspoon (1.2 g) dried herbs

1 egg

2 tablespoons (13 g) coconut flour

½ cup (250 g) marinara sauce (or Tomato Chutney, page 152)

1. Preheat your oven to 450°F (230°C, or gas mark 8).

2. Line baking sheets with parchment paper or other nonstick surface.

3. Place the cauliflower florets in a food processor and pulse until the florets are finely riced. Alternatively, you can grate the florets using a box or cheese grater.

4. Prepare a steamer and steam the riced cauliflower for about 5 minutes, or until it starts to get tender, but is not soft throughout.

5. Remove excess moisture from the steamed rice by adding it to a nut milk bag, cheesecloth, or dish towel and squeezing it over the sink. If the cauliflower is hot, wear dish-washing gloves to protect your hands.

6. Add the cauliflower, ¼ cup (22 g) of the cheese, garlic, salt, herbs, egg, and coconut flour in a mixing bowl and blend well.

7. On parchment paper or a nonstick surface, shape the mixture into a rectangle about ½-inch (1.3 cm) thick. The dough is fairly loose so use your hands to shape and flatten it. Depending on the size of your baking sheet, you may need to create two rectangles of dough.

8. Bake the dough for 15 minutes, or until the edges begin to brown. Brush the top of the dough with marinara sauce and sprinkle the remaining ¼ cup (22 g) cheese evenly across the sauce. Place back in the oven and bake until the cheese starts to bubble and brown a bit.

9. Cool for a minute, slice, and serve warm. Store sealed in the refrigerator for a few days or freeze for a few months.

Yield: 16 breadsticks

Everyday Flatbread

•Gluten-Free   •Grain-Free   •Low-Sugar

This flatbread can be used for a thin crust pizza or as bread for dipping in soups, sauces, and stews. I've used a variety of cheeses with this recipe, including mozzarella, Parmesan, aged sheep's, and aged goat's milk cheese.

2 cups (192 g) almond flour

2 tablespoons (13 g) coconut flour

½ teaspoon salt

½ teaspoon baking soda

¼ cup (60 ml) olive oil or other oil

4 large eggs

1 cup (115 g) shredded mozzarella or other cheese

1. Preheat your oven to 350°F (175°C, or gas mark 4).

2. Place the almond flour, coconut flour, salt, and baking soda in a bowl and whisk with a fork.

3. Add the oil, eggs, and cheese to the flour mixture and blend well. The dough will be slightly wet.

4. Shape the dough into one or two balls using your hands. Cover the dough and place it in the freezer for 10 minutes first. Cut two large pieces of parchment paper and place a dough ball between them. Flatten the dough a bit with your hands and then use a rolling pin to roll the dough flat until it is about ¼-inch (6 mm) thick or to your desired thickness.

5. Remove the top parchment paper and slide the rolled bread and bottom parchment paper onto a baking sheet.

6. Bake for 15 minutes, or until the edges are just starting to brown. Remove from the oven to cool.

7. Slice and serve warm or at room temperature. Store flatbread in a sealed container at room temperature for a few days, in the refrigerator for about a week, or in the freezer for a few months.

Yield: 2 flatbreads, or about 4 servings

Everyday Nut-Free Flatbread

•Gluten-Free •Grain-Free •Low-Sugar •Nut-Free

This simple nut-free flatbread can be topped with herbs, sauces, and other pizza-style toppings, or just use it as sliced wedges of bread to dip in sauces, stews, and salads. For a focaccia-style topping, try a sprinkle of coarse salt, chopped fresh rosemary, and Roasted Cherry Tomatoes (page 152).

¼ cup (26 g) coconut flour

⅛ teaspoon salt

4 large eggs

1 cup (85 g) shredded Parmesan, or mozzarella (115 g), or other cheese

1 tablespoon (15 ml) olive oil

1. Preheat your oven to 375°F (190°C, or gas mark 5).

2. Line a baking sheet with parchment paper or a nonstick mat.

3. Place the coconut flour and salt in a bowl and blend with a fork or whisk.

4. Add the eggs, cheese, and olive oil to the coconut flour mixture and blend well with a spoon or spatula. The dough will be wet.

5. Using a spatula or spoon, spread the dough out into one or two flatbreads that are about ¼-inch (6 mm) thick, or the thickness you prefer.

6. Bake for 15 minutes. If you're adding toppings, bake the bread for only 10 minutes, add the toppings, and continue baking for another 5 to 10 minutes, depending on your toppings.

7. Slice and serve warm or at room temperature. Store in a sealed container at room temperature for a few days, in the refrigerator for about a week, or in the freezer for a few months.

Yield: 1 large or 2 small flatbreads, or about 4 servings

Pesto Flatbread Pizza

•Gluten-Free   •Grain-Free   •Low-Sugar

Flatbread can have any combination of toppings you desire so take this list of ingredients as one option. One of my favorite toppings is Roasted Cherry Tomatoes (page 152) and pesto. If you don't have roasted tomatoes, use either sundried tomatoes or tomato sauce. The pesto recipe is dairy-free but, if you prefer, you can replace the pine nuts and ¼ teaspoon salt with 3 tablespoons (15 g) grated Parmesan. You can also replace the basil with fresh arugula, kale, parsley, oregano, or other mixture of fresh herbs.

One batch Everyday Flatbread (page 32)

FOR PESTO:

1 cup (20 g) packed fresh basil leaves

1 large garlic clove

3 tablespoons (25 g) pine nuts

¼ teaspoon salt

3 tablespoons (45 ml) olive oil

1 teaspoon (5 ml) lemon juice

FOR TOPPING:

1 cup (115 g) shredded mozzarella or other cheese

1 cup (150 g) Roasted Cherry Tomatoes (page 152), sun-dried tomatoes (110 g), or tomato sauce (245 g)

1. Preheat your oven to 400°F (200°C, or gas mark 6). Place prepared flatbread on a baking sheet.

2. To make the pesto: Place all the pesto ingredients in a food processor or blender and pulse until well blended.

3. Spread a thin layer of pesto on flatbread.

4. Sprinkle the cheese over the pesto, and then layer the tomatoes on top of the cheese.

5. Bake for 5 minutes, or until the cheese is as bubbly and golden as you like.

6. Cool for a moment and slice. Store pizza in a sealed container in the refrigerator for about a week or in the freezer for a few months.

Yield: 2 flatbread pizzas, or about 4 servings

Tortillas

•Gluten-Free •Grain-Free •Low-Sugar •Dairy-Free Option •Paleo •Nut-Free

Tortillas present endless meal possibilities. I use them in the Roasted Tomato and Pepper Jack Quesadillas (page 144), the Chili-Lime Chicken Quesadillas (page 143), and Mexican Lasagna (page 149). You can also let your imagination run with your favorite ingredients, or just make a simple open-faced tortilla with some beans, avocado, salsa, cheese, and a dash of hot sauce or Pico de Gallo (page 143).

Two tips to prevent these tortillas from falling apart: First, be a bit generous with the cooking oil in the skillet; and second, let them brown on the bottom and edges so it is easy to slip a spatula completely under them to flip. A little brown on the bottom is a good thing for these tortillas, and they hold together better the longer they're cooked.

For the egg whites, I usually purchase a container of organic egg whites to make a large batch of tortillas. Then I wrap the tortillas and store them in the refrigerator to have with meals during the week.

⅔ cup (155 ml) egg whites (about 4 large egg whites)

2 tablespoons (28 g) unsalted butter, melted, or ghee or coconut oil, plus more for the skillet

¼ cup (60 ml) coconut milk or other milk

1 tablespoon (15 ml) lime juice

2 tablespoons (13 g) coconut flour

¼ teaspoon ground cumin

¼ teaspoon salt

1. In a bowl, whisk together the egg whites, melted butter, milk, and lime juice.

2. Add the coconut flour, cumin, and salt to the bowl and whisk until well blended. Let the batter sit for a few minutes and mix once more.

3. Heat a skillet over medium heat and add about 2 table-spoons (28 g) unsalted butter, depending on the size of your skillet. One of the tricks to successfully making these is to always have a good layer of oil or butter in the skillet.

4. Pour about 2 tablespoons (28 ml) of batter into the skillet to make a 5-inch (13 cm) tortilla; adjust the amount of batter to make the size you prefer. Tilt the pan in a circular motion to spread the batter around in a circle.

5. Cook for a few minutes, or until the edges and bottom are browning and you can easily slip a spatula under it, then flip the tortilla to the other side. Cook for another minute or so and transfer to a warm plate. Continue with the remaining batter.

6. Serve warm. Store in a sealed container in the refrigerator for a few days or in the freezer for a few months.

Yield: 6 tortillas

Skillet Corn Bread

•Gluten-Free   •Dairy-Free Option   •Low-Sugar   •Nut-Free

A really good reason to make corn bread in a skillet is that the butter added to the hot skillet makes for a nice crispy bottom and edges. I usually use an 8-inch (20 cm) skillet for this recipe, but a 10-inch (25 cm) skillet works, too, resulting in a slightly lower profile corn bread. If you prefer, you can bake this corn bread in a small baking pan (follow the baking directions for Cinnamon Berry Corn Bread on page 40). You can also use this batter to bake corn bread muffins, which will yield 6 muffins.

The bottom of this corn bread is crisp when warm out of the oven but softens as it cools. To crisp it again, toast a slice of corn bread for a few minutes. If you want it very crisp, bordering on burnt (as I like it), let the batter cook in the skillet over medium-high heat for about 1 minute before transferring it to the oven.

3 tablespoons (42 g) unsalted butter or ghee, palm shortening, or coconut oil), divided

3 large eggs

3 tablespoons (60 g) maple syrup or honey

¼ teaspoon vanilla extract

½ teaspoon salt

¼ teaspoon baking soda

3 tablespoons (18 g) cornmeal (gluten-free; see Resources, page 154)

2 tablespoons (13 g) coconut flour

1. Preheat your oven to 400°F (200°C, or gas mark 6).

2. Melt 2 tablespoons (28 g) of the butter. Pour the butter into a medium-size bowl. Add the eggs, maple syrup, and vanilla and whisk together.

3. Add the salt, baking soda, cornmeal, and coconut flour to the wet ingredients and blend well with a whisk. Let the batter sit for a few minutes and blend once more.

4. Warm a skillet on medium-high heat and melt the remaining 1 tablespoon (14 g) butter until it sizzles.

5. Pour the batter into the skillet, transfer the skillet to the oven, and bake for 10 minutes, or until a toothpick inserted in the center comes out clean.

6. Slice and serve warm or at room temperature. Store in a sealed container at room temperature for a few days, in the refrigerator for a few weeks, or in the freezer for a few months.

Yield: 6 to 8 servings

Cinnamon Berry Corn Bread

•Gluten-Free •Dairy-Free Option •Nut-Free

Here's a sweet take on corn bread using berries and cinnamon. You can make this bread in a skillet (follow the baking directions for Skillet Corn Bread on page 39), or bake it in a 6 × 6 × 2-inch (15 × 15 × 5 cm) baking pan, or for a thinner bread use an 8 × 8 × 2-inch (20 × 20 × 5 cm) baking pan.

3 large eggs

2 tablespoons (28 g) unsalted butter, melted, or ghee, palm shortening, or coconut oil

3 tablespoons (60 g) maple syrup or honey

¼ teaspoon vanilla extract

½ teaspoon salt

¼ teaspoon baking soda

1 teaspoon (2 g) ground cinnamon

3 tablespoons (18 g) cornmeal (gluten-free; see Resources, page 154)

2 tablespoons (13 g) coconut flour

1 cup (150 g) blueberries or other berries

1. Preheat your oven to 400°F (200°C, or gas mark 6).

2. In a medium-size bowl, whisk together the eggs, butter, maple syrup, and vanilla.

3. Add the salt, baking soda, cinnamon, cornmeal, and coconut flour to the wet ingredients and stir until well blended. Fold in the blueberries. Let the batter sit for a few minutes and blend once more.

4. Generously grease a 6 × 6 × 2-inch (15 × 15 × 5 cm) baking pan and pour the corn bread batter into the pan.

5. Bake for 12 minutes, or until a toothpick inserted in the center of the corn bread comes out clean.

6. Slice and serve warm or at room temperature. Store in a sealed container at room temperature for a few days, in the refrigerator for a few weeks, or in the freezer for a few months.

Yield: 6 to 8 servings

Drop Biscuits

•Gluten-Free   •Grain-Free   •Dairy-Free Option   •Low-Sugar   •Paleo   •Nut-Free

You might think it unreasonable to get tender, savory biscuits using coconut flour, but add the right amount of moisture and butter, and it's biscuits and gravy time. This basic biscuit recipe can accompany a soup, stew, or you can just snack on them with a smear of jam or butter (omit herbs if so).

You can use any kind of milk in this recipe, dairy or dairy-free, or make it richer by trying cream, sour cream, or yogurt instead of the milk. And if you're finding these biscuits a bit on the dry side, add another tablespoon of milk or even water.

4 eggs

¼ cup (57 g) unsalted butter, melted, or coconut oil, lard, or palm shortening

1¼ cups (300 ml) coconut milk or other milk

¼ teaspoon salt

¼ teaspoon baking soda

⅔ cup (70 g) coconut flour

1 tablespoon (2.5 g) chopped fresh herbs such as basil, oregano, parsley, or thyme (optional)

1. Preheat your oven to 350°F (180°C, or gas mark 4).

2. Generously grease a baking sheet, or line it with parchment paper or a nonstick mat.

3. Using a whisk or handheld mixer, mix together the eggs, butter, milk, salt, baking soda, and herbs until well blended.

4. Add the coconut flour to the batter and mix until well blended and all lumps are gone. Let the batter sit for a few minutes and mix again. The batter should be mushy and easy to spoon and drop onto the baking sheet. If you find it's too stiff, add another tablespoon of coconut milk or water.

5. Spoon about 2 tablespoons (42 g) of batter for each biscuit onto the greased baking sheet.

6. Bake for 20 minutes or until the biscuits are tender but firm. Serve warm or at room temperature. Store in a sealed container in the refrigerator for a few days or in the freezer for a few months. For leftovers, reheat or toast for a few minutes to serve warm.

Yield: 12 biscuits

Cheddar Biscuits

•Gluten-Free   •Grain-Free   •Low-Sugar   •Nut-Free

This drop biscuit is moist and savory thanks to the cheddar cheese. Cheddar and butter make excellent flavoring for this simple biscuit, and these can be reheated or toasted for a few minutes to serve warm.

4 large eggs

¼ cup (57 g) cup unsalted butter, melted, or coconut oil, lard, or palm shortening

1¼ cups (300 ml) coconut milk or other milk

¼ teaspoon salt

¼ teaspoon baking soda

¼ teaspoon garlic powder

½ cup (56 g) finely shredded or grated sharp cheddar cheese

1 tablespoon (4 g) fresh oregano, basil, or other herbs (optional)

⅔ cup (70 g) coconut flour

1. Preheat your oven to 350°F (180°C, or gas mark 4).

2. Generously grease a baking sheet, or line it with parchment paper or a nonstick mat.

3. Using a handheld or stand mixer, mix together the eggs, butter, milk, salt, baking soda, garlic powder, cheese, and herbs until well blended.

4. Add the coconut flour to the batter and mix until well blended and all the lumps are gone. Let the batter sit for a few minutes and mix again. The batter should be mushy and easy to spoon and drop onto the baking sheet. If you find it's too stiff, add another tablespoon of coconut milk or water.

5. Spoon about 2 tablespoons (42 g) of batter for each biscuit onto the greased baking sheet.

6. Bake for 25 minutes or until the biscuits are tender but firm.

7. Serve warm or at room temperature. Store in a sealed container in the refrigerator for a few days or in the freezer for a few months. For leftovers, reheat or toast for a few minutes to serve warm.

Yield: 12 biscuits

Chocolate Zucchini Bread

•Gluten-Free •Grain-Free •Dairy-Free Option •Paleo •Nut-Free

Here's a chocolate take on zucchini bread. Not too dense, this gluten-free chocolate zucchini bread is moist, dark, and subtly sweet. You can bake it either as a quick-cake or as a bread.

Some of this bread's sweetness comes from sweetened chocolate chips, but if you don't want to add them, it is still sweet on its own. If you find it's not sweet enough, you can add another tablespoon of maple syrup or a bit of another sweetener, such as a drop of liquid stevia, a pinch of powdered stevia, or 1 teaspoon (2.5 g) of coconut sugar. Another nice addition is ½ teaspoon of ground cinnamon, and if you want a bit of a kick in the flavor, add ½ teaspoon of chili powder.

The key to using zucchini in this recipe and others is to remove any excess moisture. To do this, place the zucchini in a towel and squeeze.

This recipe is quite flexible, so feel free to bake it in a loaf pan as a bread, a square baking pan to make cake squares, or a muffin pan to have cupcakes (these will bake a little faster than as a bread or cake). It's up to you.

2 cups (200 g) grated or finely shredded zucchini (about 1 zucchini)

4 large eggs

2 tablespoons (30 ml) olive oil or unsalted butter, ghee, or coconut oil

⅓ cup (106 g) maple syrup or honey

1 teaspoon of vanilla extract

⅓ cup (35 g) coconut flour

¼ cup (20 g) unsweetened cocoa powder

½ teaspoon baking soda

½ teaspoon salt

⅓ cup (56 g) chocolate chips

1. Preheat your oven to 350°F (180°C, or gas mark 4).

2. Grease the baking pan and line the bottom with parchment paper. Dust the sides with coconut flour. If you want easy release, line the entire pan with parchment paper.

3. If your zucchini is too moist, wring out the excess moisture by placing the zucchini in a towel and squeezing.

4. Using a food processor or mixer, blend together the zucchini, eggs, oil, maple syrup, and vanilla. A food processor will further break up the zucchini so you won't see it in the baked bread.

5. Add the flour, cocoa, baking soda, and salt to the zucchini mixture and stir until well blended. Let the batter sit for a few minutes.

6. Mix in the chocolate chips then pour the batter into the prepared pan and bake for 45 to 50 minutes, or until a toothpick inserted in the center comes out clean.

7. Cool and serve. Store, covered, at room temperature for several days or in the refrigerator for a few weeks.

Yield: 1 loaf

Chocolate Banana Bread

•Gluten-Free •Grain-Free •Dairy-Free •Paleo

This recipe is a bit of a riff on my classic banana bread but using almond and coconut flour. The original recipe doesn't use the shaved chocolate. This bread bakes to the top of a 7.5 × 3.5 × 2.25-inch (19 × 9 × 6 cm) loaf pan, so any pan around these dimensions or a bit larger will work.

I usually use a coffee grinder to grind chocolate chips into chocolate powder, but you could use a vegetable peeler, hand grater, or box grater to shave a chunk of your favorite chocolate. Grating it into a powder distributes the chocolate throughout the loaf; however, feel free to just load up chocolate chips or chunks of chocolate, if you prefer.

¾ cup (72 g) almond flour

¼ cup (26 g) coconut flour

¾ teaspoon baking soda

½ teaspoon salt

2 tablespoons (30 ml) olive oil or other oil

3 large eggs

1 cup (250 g) mashed banana (about 2 very ripe bananas)

¼ cup (80 g) maple syrup or honey

½ cup (52 g) finely shaved or ground dark chocolate

1. Preheat your oven to 350°F (180°C, or gas mark 4).

2. Prepare a baking pan by greasing it generously or lining the bottom with parchment paper and greasing the sides.

3. Whisk the almond flour, coconut flour, baking soda, and salt together in a bowl.

4. Add the olive oil, eggs, bananas, maple syrup, and chocolate to the dry ingredients and blend well with a stand or handheld mixer. Let the batter sit for a few minutes and mix once more.

5. Spoon the batter into the baking pan and bake for 45 minutes, or until a toothpick inserted in the middle of the bread comes out clean.

6. Cool and slice. Store the bread, covered, at room temperature for a few days, the refrigerator for a few weeks, or in the freezer for a few months.

Yield: 1 loaf

Spiced Pumpkin Bread

•Gluten-Free　•Grain-Free　•Dairy-Free　•Low-Sugar Option　•Paleo

This pumpkin bread boasts an array of spices, including nutmeg, ginger, cinnamon, and cloves, that have natural anti-inflammatory properties. I use a 7.5 × 3.5 × 2.25-inch (19 × 9 × 6 cm) loaf pan, but you can use a slightly larger pan for a lower profile loaf. This is not a heavy bread, so a thin layer of either the Maple Cream Cheese Frosting (page 101) or the Maple Cream Frosting (page 101) for a dairy-free option goes well on the top of the bread, once it has cooled.

To make this low-sugar, replace ¼ cup (80 g) of the maple syrup or honey with 20 drops of liquid stevia or 1 teaspoon (2.5 g) powdered stevia. Another option is to replace the full ½ cup (160 g) with ¼ cup (30 g) coconut sugar and ¼ cup (60 ml) coconut milk or other milk.

½ cup (120 g) pumpkin or butternut squash purée (canned or freshly roasted—see page 131 for roasting directions)

½ cup (160 g) maple syrup or honey

4 large eggs

¼ teaspoon baking soda

¼ teaspoon salt

½ teaspoon ground nutmeg

½ teaspoon ground cinnamon

½ teaspoon ground cloves

½ teaspoon ground ginger

¼ cup plus 2 tablespoons (39 g) coconut flour

1. Preheat your oven to 350°F (180°C, or gas mark 4).

2. Prepare a baking pan by greasing it generously or lining the bottom with parchment paper and greasing the sides.

3. Add the squash, maple syrup, and eggs to a medium-size bowl and blend well.

4. Add the baking soda, salt, nutmeg, cinnamon, cloves, ginger, and coconut flour to the wet mixture and use a handheld or stand mixer to blend well. Let the batter sit for few minutes and mix once more.

5. Transfer the batter to the baking pan and bake for 40 minutes, or until a toothpick inserted in the center comes out clean.

6. Cool and frost. Store in a sealed container at room temperature for a few days, in the refrigerator for a few weeks, or in the freezer for a few months.

Yield: 1 loaf

Banana Bread

•Gluten-Free   •Grain-Free   •Dairy-Free   •Low-Sugar Option   •Paleo

This is a light, moist, banana bread—lighter than most other moist breads thanks to the coconut flour. To make this low-sugar, don't add the maple syrup or honey—it will still be sweet! If you're finding it is too moist, add an additional teaspoon or so of coconut flour to the batter.

Some coconut flour baking recipes taste best when allowed to cool at room temperature for an hour or so, and this bread definitely benefits from cooling time. I recommend cooling your loaf at least an hour before slicing and serving.

1½ cups (300 g) mashed banana (about 3 ripe bananas)

2 tablespoons (40 g) maple syrup or honey

3 large eggs

1 tablespoon (15 ml) vanilla extract

¾ teaspoon baking soda

½ teaspoon salt

¼ cup plus 2 tablespoons (39 g) coconut flour

1. Preheat your oven to 350°F (180°C, or gas mark 4).

2. Line a 7.5 × 3.5 × 2.5-inch (19 × 9 × 6 cm) loaf pan with parchment paper, or grease it generously.

3. Add the mashed bananas, maple syrup, eggs, and vanilla extract to a large bowl and blend well.

4. Add the baking soda, salt, and coconut flour to the wet batter and blend well. Let the batter sit for 5 minutes to give the coconut flour time to absorb the liquids.

5. Pour the batter into the baking pan and bake for 55 minutes, or until the top begins to brown and a toothpick inserted in the center of the bread comes out clean.

6. Cool and slice. Store, covered, at room temperature for a few days, in the refrigerator for a few weeks, or in the freezer for a few months.

Yield: 1 loaf

CHAPTER 3

WAFFLES, PANCAKES, MUFFINS, AND DONUTS

From savory Mushroom Feta Spinach Crêpes (page 76) to Morning Glory Muffins (page 65) and Caramel Vanilla Donuts (page 69), this chapter showcases an array of snack and meal ideas. While you might certainly think of crêpes, muffins, and donuts as breakfast treats, these recipes make great everyday snacks since they're loaded with protein, good fat, and fiber. And who doesn't love having pancakes or hash brown waffles for dinner?!

Savory Waffles

•Gluten-Free •Grain-Free •Low-Sugar •Nut-Free

These savory waffles make a great base for a meal. Add some grilled chicken or chopped ham or bacon, sliced avocados, a few diced tomatoes, and salad dressing and you have a meal. Or try adding a fried egg and some salsa. For the pepper Jack cheese, feel free to substitute Monterey Jack or other savory cheese. If you use a mellow cheese, you might want to add a bit more salt or maybe a dash of hot sauce to the batter.

4 large eggs

1 teaspoon (5 ml) olive oil or other oil

½ cup (56 g) trimmed and finely sliced scallions (about 3 onions)

¾ cup (100 g) grated pepper Jack cheese or other cheese

¼ teaspoon baking soda

Pinch salt (less than ⅛ teaspoon)

2 tablespoons (13 g) coconut flour

1. Preheat your waffle iron to a medium heat.

2. Mix all the ingredients together using a mixer or whisk. Let the batter sit for a few minutes and mix once more.

3. Scoop ½ cup to 1 cup (120 to 235 ml) batter, depending on the size of your waffle iron, and pour onto the iron. Cook the waffle on medium heat, following the manufacturer's directions.

4. Serve warm. The waffles can be stored in a sealed container in the refrigerator for about a week or in the freezer for a few months.

Yield: About 4 large waffles

Banana Bread Waffles

•Gluten-Free   •Grain-Free   •Dairy-Free   •Paleo

This is my popular recipe for banana bread and is loved by so many, but I discovered that it also makes great waffles, made even more decadent when you add chocolate chips or blueberries. I personally don't see the need for syrup with these waffles, but I'll leave that decision up to you. And you can always make a loaf of banana bread or muffins if you don't have a waffle iron.

¾ teaspoon baking soda

½ teaspoon salt

¾ cup (72 g) almond flour

¼ cup (26 g) coconut flour

2 tablespoons (28 ml) olive oil or other oil

3 large eggs

1 cup (250 g) mashed banana (about 2 very ripe bananas)

¼ cup (80 g) maple syrup or honey

½ cup (84 g) chocolate chips, or ½ cup (75 g) blueberries (optional)

1. Preheat the waffle iron.

2. Using a whisk or handheld mixer, mix together the baking soda, salt, almond flour, and coconut flour until well blended.

3. Add the oil, eggs, banana, and maple syrup to the dry mixture and blend well with a mixer. Let the batter sit for a few minutes, add the chocolate chips or blueberries, and mix gently to blend.

4. Scoop ½ cup to 1 cup (120 to 235 ml) batter, depending on the size of your waffle iron, and pour onto the iron. Cook the waffle on medium heat, following the manufacturer's directions. Transfer the waffle to a warm plate and repeat until all the batter has been used.

5. Serve warm. Store the waffles in a sealed container in the refrigerator for a few days or in the freezer for a few months.

Yield: About 8 waffles

Churro Waffles

•Gluten-Free   •Grain-Free   •Dairy-Free Option   •Low-Sugar   •Paleo

Whip up a simple batch of waffles with this recipe and then add a cinnamon-sugar-butter coating—no need for maple syrup or other sweet topping. I use coconut sugar for the topping but feel free to use whole cane sugar. If you're avoiding sugar altogether, dip each waffle in melted butter and then sprinkle on some cinnamon and drizzle some honey or maple syrup on top.

The size of your waffle iron will determine how many waffles you actually yield from this recipe, but I'd say if you're serving more than two people double the recipe.

To make this dairy-free, substitute coconut oil for the butter in the topping.

FOR WAFFLES:

4 large eggs

1 teaspoon (5 ml) olive oil or other oil

1 teaspoon (5 ml) vanilla extract

¼ teaspoon baking soda

¼ teaspoon ground cinnamon

1 teaspoon (7 g) honey or maple syrup

2 tablespoons (13 g) coconut flour

FOR CINNAMON-SUGAR TOPPING:

½ cup (60 g) coconut sugar or maple sugar

2 tablespoons (14 g) ground cinnamon

¼ cup (57 g) unsalted butter (or coconut oil or palm shortening)

1. Preheat your waffle iron to a medium heat.

2. To make the waffles: Mix together the eggs, oil, vanilla, baking soda, cinnamon, honey, and coconut flour using a mixer, food processor, or whisk. Let the batter sit for a few minutes and mix once more.

3. Scoop the batter onto the iron. Cook according to manufacturer's directions.

4. To make the topping: Mix the coconut sugar and cinnamon together and place on a plate as large as your waffles. Melt the butter and pour into a wide bowl or plate as large as your waffles.

5. While the waffles are warm, dip each waffle in the butter, turn, and dip the other side, and then dip each side in the cinnamon sugar mixture.

6. Serve warm or at room temperature. To make these for a later date, make the topping when you are ready to serve the waffles. Store the waffles (no topping) in a sealed container in the refrigerator for about a week or in the freezer for a few months.

Yield: About 4 large waffles

Hash Brown Waffles

•Gluten-Free •Grain-Free •Dairy-Free •Low-Sugar •Nut-Free

Here's another savory waffle using grated potatoes and a bit of coconut flour to absorb some of the excess moisture from the potatoes. You can use either a box grater or the grating attachment of a food processor to grate the potatoes and onion, but the key to good hash brown waffles is to squeeze as much moisture out of the grated potatoes and onions as possible before mixing them in with the other ingredients.

I season mine with just salt but feel free to add your own touch, such as some garlic powder, cayenne, and black pepper. The waffles make a great base for a meal. Try topping your waffles with spinach and scrambled eggs, salsa, and some hot sauce. Or serve them alongside a sausage-and-apple stir-fry, or simply dip them in ketchup or gravy.

3 medium russet potatoes, about 1½ pounds (680 g), unpeeled and grated

1 tablespoon (7 g) coconut flour

½ medium yellow onion, grated

1 tablespoon (15 ml) sunflower oil (or coconut oil or other cooking oil)

1 large egg

1 teaspoon salt

1. Preheat your waffle iron. Spray or rub some cooking oil on the inside of the waffle iron, even if it's a nonstick surface.

2. Press all the excess liquid out of the onion and potato shreds. I do this by placing them on a kitchen towel and wringing the liquid out.

3. Mix the potato, coconut flour, onion, oil, egg, and salt together in a bowl.

4. Follow the directions for using your waffle iron to make the waffles. I generally scoop about ½ cup (106 g) of the potato mixture for each waffle and cook it on a very high setting. Let the waffle turn dark so that it crisps on the outside and is easy to remove from the waffle iron.

5. Serve warm. Store in a sealed container in the refrigerator for a few days or in the freezer for a few months.

Yield: 4 to 6 waffles

Chocolate Chip Scones

•Gluten-Free   •Grain-Free   •Dairy-Free Option
•Paleo   •Nut-Free

Scones pair well with your relaxing morning cup of tea or coffee, but they are also a great on-the-run breakfast meal or snack. These chocolate chip scones are a bit on the lighter side, as far as scones go, thanks to the lightness of coconut flour. This recipe makes a good number of scones, so stash some away in the freezer for a later date.

To make these dairy-free, for the yogurt substitute coconut milk or other dairy-free yogurt or cream.

4 large eggs

¼ cup (57 g) unsalted butter, melted, or coconut oil, ghee, or palm shortening

¾ cup (173 g) plain yogurt, crème frâiche, or sour cream

¼ cup (80 g) maple syrup or honey

½ teaspoon salt

½ teaspoon baking soda

¾ cup (78 g) coconut flour

½ cup (84 g) chocolate chips

1. Preheat your oven to 350°F (180°C, or gas mark 4).

2. Generously grease a baking sheet, or line it with parchment paper or nonstick mat.

3. Add the eggs, butter, yogurt, maple syrup, salt, and baking soda to a bowl and mix, using a handheld or stand mixer, until well blended.

4. Add the coconut flour to the batter and mix until well blended. Stir in the chocolate chips. Let the batter sit for a few minutes and mix again. The batter should be mushy and easy to spoon and drop onto the baking sheet. If you find it's still too stiff, add another tablespoon of coconut milk or water.

5. For each scone, spoon between 1 to 2 tablespoons (about 42 g) of batter onto the baking sheet and shape it a bit with your fingers or a spoon.

6. Bake for 25 minutes or until the biscuits are browning on the bottom and edges and are a bit tender to touch.

7. Cool and serve warm or at room temperature. Store in a sealed container at room temperature for a few days or in the freezer for a few months.

Yield: 16 to 20 scones

Silver Dollar Pancakes

•Gluten-Free •Grain-Free •Dairy-Free •Low-Sugar
•Paleo •Nut-Free

Make these pancakes the size of silver dollars (on the small side) by dropping about a tablespoon of batter on a skillet for each one. You can make them larger by using about 2 tablespoons (about 22 g) and pouring it around or tilting the pan around in a circle to spread the batter. If you're finding your pancakes taste a bit too much like an omelet ("too eggy") try adding about ½ to 1 tablespoon (4 to 7 g) more of coconut flour. This can make the difference for some folks.

3 large eggs

1 teaspoon (5 ml) high-heat cooking oil, ghee, or coconut oil, plus more for cooking

½ teaspoon vanilla extract

1 teaspoon (7 g) honey or maple syrup

¼ teaspoon ground cinnamon (optional)

¼ teaspoon baking soda

⅛ teaspoon salt

2 tablespoons (13 g) coconut flour

1. Whisk together the eggs, 1 teaspoon (5 ml) oil, the vanilla, and the honey.

2. Add the cinnamon, baking soda, salt, and coconut flour to the wet ingredients, and whisk until well blended. Let the batter sit for a few minutes so the coconut flour can absorb the moisture, then whisk again to remove any remaining lumps.

3. Preheat a skillet on low to medium heat. Add a generous amount of cooking oil to coat the entire skillet.

4. Pour about 1 tablespoon (11 g) of batter for each pancake in the skillet without letting the edges of the pancakes touch. Let the pancakes cook slowly to avoid burning the bottoms. Flip the pancakes after a few minutes or when the edges begin to brown and you can easily slide a spatula under the pancake. They will take a bit longer to cook on each side than the average pancake. Repeat for the remaining batter, adding more cooking oil as necessary. Serve warm.

Yield: About 12 silver dollar-size pancakes, or about 3 servings

Cinnamon Bun Muffins

•Gluten-Free •Grain-Free •Dairy-Free Option •Low-Sugar Option •Paleo

Cinnamon bun muffins came out of my desire for a sweet muffin that resembled the flavor of cinnamon buns but without the yeast and preparation time. These muffins are an all-time favorite in my home and in many others and can withstand a number of substitutions. For butter you can use coconut oil. For the honey in the muffin batter, you can replace it with ½ teaspoon stevia plus ½ cup (120 ml) milk or dairy-free milk. For the topping, you can substitute coconut sugar for the honey or try ¼ teaspoon of stevia with chopped pecans.

FOR MUFFINS:

½ cup (52 g) coconut flour

¼ teaspoon baking soda

¼ teaspoon salt

4 large eggs

⅓ cup (77 g) yogurt, coconut milk or other milk

½ cup (170 g) maple syrup or honey

FOR CINNAMON TOPPING:

2 tablespoons (14 g) ground cinnamon

¼ cup (80 g) honey, maple syrup, or other sweetener

2 tablespoons (28 g) unsalted butter, melted, or coconut oil

½ cup (56 g) chopped pecans or walnuts (optional)

1. Preheat oven to 350°F (180°C, or gas mark 4).

2. To make the muffins: Whisk the coconut flour, baking soda, and salt together in a bowl.

3. Add the eggs, yogurt, and maple syrup to the dry mixture and blend well with a mixer or by hand with a large spoon. Let the batter sit for a few minutes.

4. To make the topping: Place the cinnamon, honey, butter, and pecans in a small bowl and mix together with a fork or whisk.

5. To assemble: Fill muffin liners or silicon cups about one-quarter of the way with batter. Spoon about a tablespoon (27 g) of the topping over each muffin, and then top off each one with more batter, up to three-quarters of the way full. Drizzle the remaining topping over each muffin. Use a toothpick, fork, or spoon to gently blend the topping into the muffin batter.

6. Bake the muffins for about 20 minutes, or until a toothpick inserted in the center of the muffin comes out clean.

7. Store, covered, for a few days at room temperature, in the refrigerator for a few weeks, or in the freezer for a few months.

Yield: 8 muffins

Pumpkin Muffins

•Gluten-Free   •Grain-Free   •Dairy-Free   •Paleo

Here's a simple pumpkin muffin that can be made as regular-size muffins or mini-muffins. Like many muffin recipes using coconut flour, this one is light and works well with a variety of spices and sweeteners. You can use canned pumpkin here, or freshly roasted squash. My favorite squash purée is roasted butternut squash (page 131).

½ cup (120 g) butternut squash or pumpkin purée

½ cup (160 g) of maple syrup or honey

4 large eggs

¼ teaspoon baking soda

¼ teaspoon salt

½ teaspoon ground nutmeg

½ teaspoon ground cinnamon

½ teaspoon ground cloves

½ teaspoon ground ginger

¼ cup plus 2 tablespoons (39 g) coconut flour

1. Preheat your oven to 350°F (180°C, or gas mark 4).

2. Prepare a muffin pan by lining the muffin wells with liners. Grease the liners as well unless they are nonstick liners.

3. Place the purée, honey, and eggs in a bowl and blend well. I use a mixer for this batter.

4. Add the baking soda, salt, nutmeg, cinnamon, cloves, ginger, and coconut flour to the wet ingredients and mix well. Let the batter sit for a few minutes and then mix again.

5. Fill the muffin liners two-thirds full and bake for 15 minutes, or until a toothpick inserted in the center of a muffin comes out clean.

6. Cool and serve. Store in a sealed container at room temperature for a few days, in the refrigerator for a few weeks, or in the freezer for a few months.

Yield: 8 muffins

Banana-Blueberry Muffins

•Gluten-Free •Grain-Free •Dairy-Free •Low-Sugar •Paleo

This muffin is sweetened primarily with bananas and some maple syrup added to finish it. You can use frozen berries if blueberries are not in season. I buy a lot of blueberries when they're in season with the intent of freezing a couple of pints. Other berries, such as blackberries and huckleberries, work well in this muffin, too. For a low-sugar option, reduce the maple syrup to 2 tablespoons (40 g).

¾ cup (72 g) almond flour

¼ cup (26 g) coconut flour

¾ teaspoon baking soda

½ teaspoon salt

2 tablespoons (28 ml) olive oil or other oil

3 large eggs

1 cup (250 g) mashed banana (about 2 very ripe bananas)

¼ cup (80 g) maple syrup or honey

½ cup (75 g) fresh or frozen blueberries

1. Preheat your oven to 350°F (180°C, or gas mark 4).

2. Prepare a muffin pan with muffin liners.

3. Whisk the almond flour, coconut flour, baking soda, and salt together in a bowl.

4. Add the olive oil, eggs, bananas, and maple syrup to the dry ingredients and blend well with a stand or handheld mixer. Let the batter sit for a few minutes and mix once more. Gently mix in the blueberries.

5. Fill the muffin liners three-quarters of the way and bake for 25 minutes, or until a toothpick inserted in the middle of a muffin comes out clean.

6. Cool and slice. Store, covered, at room temperature for a few days, in the refrigerator for a few weeks, or in the freezer for a few months.

Yield: 8 muffins

Morning Glory Muffins

•Gluten-Free •Grain-Free •Dairy-Free Option •Paleo
•Nut-Free

This recipe came to me while testing carrot cake and thinking about a Comfy Belly reader's request for a grain-free muffin. I played around with the ratio of the ingredients.

Note that if you soak the dates in hot water for 10 minutes, then drain them, it will be easier to blend them into the rest of the batter.

3 ounces (80 g) Medjool dates (about 4 dates), pitted

1 cup (70 g) shredded raw carrots

1 cup (86 g) peeled, shredded apple

¼ cup (57 g) unsalted butter, melted, or coconut oil, palm shortening, or ghee

¼ cup (60 ml) coconut milk or other dairy-free milk

4 large eggs

¼ cup (80 g) maple syrup or honey

1 teaspoon (5 ml) vanilla extract

¼ cup plus 1 tablespoon (33 g) coconut flour

1 teaspoon (2 g) ground cinnamon

½ teaspoon ground nutmeg

¼ teaspoon ground cloves

½ teaspoon baking soda

½ teaspoon salt

¼ cup (30 g) chopped walnuts (optional)

¼ cup (30 g) golden raisins or other raisins (optional)

1. Preheat oven to 350°F (180°C, or gas mark 4).

2. Place the dates in a food processor and pulse to chop them up and create a paste. Alternatively, you can use a knife to chop them into small pieces.

3. Drain any excess liquid from the carrots and apples and place in a mixing bowl. Add the dates, butter, milk, eggs, maple syrup, and vanilla and blend well. I use a mixer for this step, but you can mix by hand as well.

4. In a separate bowl, whisk together the coconut flour, cinnamon, nutmeg, cloves, baking soda, and salt. Add the dry mix to the wet mix and blend well. Stir in the walnuts and raisins.

5. Line muffin tins with liners and fill each almost to the top with muffin batter. These muffins don't rise much at all. Bake for 25 minutes, or until a toothpick inserted in the middle of a muffin comes out clean.

6. Cool and serve. Store in a sealed container at room temperature for a few days, in the refrigerator for a few weeks, or in the freezer for a few months.

Yield: 8 muffins

Vanilla Chocolate Chip Muffins

•Gluten-Free   •Grain-Free   •Dairy-Free Option   •Low-Sugar Option   •Paleo   •Nut-Free

I enjoy chocolate added to just about any treat, and of course chocolate is a treat itself. So here are simple muffins with chocolate chips. It's really more of a cake or cupcake, but that won't stop you from eating them any time of day.

You can make this low-sugar by replacing ¼ cup (80 g) of the honey or maple syrup with ¼ cup (60 ml) coconut milk and ½ teaspoon of powdered stevia.

½ cup (52 g) coconut flour

¼ teaspoon baking soda

¼ teaspoon salt

4 large eggs

⅓ cup (76 g) unsalted butter, melted, or coconut oil, ghee, olive oil, or cooking oil

½ cup (170 g) honey or maple syrup

1 tablespoon (15 ml) vanilla extract

2 tablespoons (28 ml) coconut milk or other milk

⅓ cup (56 g) chocolate chips or mini chocolate chips (see Resources, page 154)

1. Preheat your oven to 350°F (180°C, or gas mark 4).

2. Add the coconut flour, baking soda, and salt to a large bowl and blend well.

3. Add the eggs, butter, honey, vanilla, and coconut milk to the dry ingredients and use a handheld or stand mixer to blend well. Gently stir in the chocolate chips, using a spoon or spatula.

4. Line muffin tins and fill about three-quarters of the way with batter. Bake for 20 minutes, or until a toothpick inserted in the center of a cupcake comes out clean.

5. Cool and frost. Store the cupcakes, covered, at room temperature for a few days, in the refrigerator for a few weeks, or in the freezer for a few months.

Yield: 8 muffins

Chocolate Donuts

•Gluten-Free •Grain-Free •Dairy-Free Option •Paleo •Nut-Free

I favor the old-fashioned cake style of donut. I usually make these in a regular-size donut pan that bakes in the oven, but you can also use an electric donut maker or mini-donut maker to whip up a batch of these delightful treats. Or just make them as cupcakes and top with caramel topping (page 69), Chocolate Ganache (page 96), or Simple Chocolate Frosting (page 98). Another option is to first dip the donut tops in warmed honey and then dip them in toasted coconut (page 81).

½ cup (52 g) coconut flour

¼ teaspoon salt

¼ teaspoon baking soda

¼ cup (20 g) unsweetened cocoa

6 large eggs

½ cup (170 g) maple syrup or honey

1 tablespoon (15 ml) vanilla extract

½ cup plus 1 tablespoon (126 g) unsalted butter, melted, or coconut oil, ghee, or palm shortening

1. Preheat your oven to 350°F (180°C, or gas mark 4).

2. Generously grease the donut pan or follow the instructions for your donut maker.

3. Blend the flour, salt, baking soda, and cocoa together in a bowl.

4. Add the eggs, maple syrup, vanilla, and butter to the dry ingredients and mix using a handheld or stand mixer. Let the batter sit for a few minutes and mix once more.

5. Fill the donut pan wells about two-thirds of the way with batter.

6. Bake for 20 minutes, or until a toothpick inserted in the center of a donut comes out clean.

7. Cool and serve. Store in a sealed container for a few days at room temperature, in the refrigerator for a few weeks, or in the freezer for a few months.

Yield: 8 donuts

Caramel Vanilla Donuts

•Gluten-Free   •Grain-Free   •Dairy-Free Option   •Paleo   •Nut-Free Option

Caramel and vanilla donuts go perfectly together. This recipe works with any kind or size of donut pan, including a donut baking pan for your oven, an electric donut maker, or a mini-donut maker.

For the caramel sauce, you can substitute a different nut butter if you prefer, or a seed butter if you're avoiding nuts. To make this dairy-free, use either coconut oil or palm shortening in place of butter.

FOR VANILLA DONUTS:

½ cup (52 g) coconut flour

½ teaspoon baking soda

¼ teaspoon salt

¼ teaspoon ground cinnamon

4 large eggs

¼ cup (57 g) unsalted butter, ghee, coconut oil, or palm shortening

¼ cup (60 ml) coconut milk or other milk

¼ cup (80 g) honey or maple syrup

1 tablespoon (15 ml) vanilla extract

1 teaspoon (5 ml) lemon juice

FOR CARAMEL TOPPING:

¼ cup (80 g) honey

1 tablespoon (16 g) unsalted roasted creamy almond butter or other nut or seed butter

¼ teaspoon salt

1. Preheat your oven to 350°F (180°C, or gas mark 4).

2. Grease your donut pan (or follow the directions for your donut maker).

3. To make the donuts: Place the coconut flour, baking soda, salt, and cinnamon in a bowl and blend well.

4. Add the eggs, butter, milk, honey, vanilla, and lemon juice to a separate mixing bowl and blend well.

5. Add the dry mix to the wet mix and blend well using a handheld or stand mixer. Let the batter stand for a few minutes and mix once more.

6. Fill the donut pan or maker with batter so it reaches the top of the donut well. To make it easy to fill the donut pan, place the batter in a resealable plastic bag, cut a small piece from one corner, and pipe the batter into the donut wells.

7. Bake the donuts for 15 minutes for regular-size donuts, or until a toothpick inserted in the center of the donut comes out clean. If using an electric donut maker, follow directions there.

8. Cool the donuts.

9. To make the caramel topping: Place the honey in a small saucepan and bring to a soft boil on a medium-low heat for 5 minutes, or until the honey is bubbling and turns darker but doesn't burn.

10. Turn the heat off and add the almond butter and salt. Stir until well blended. As the mixture cools it will get thicker.

11. Drizzle about 2 teaspoons (14 g) of caramel over each donut. Cool and serve.

Yield: 8 regular donuts or 24 mini-donuts

Cinnamon Sugar Donuts

•Gluten-Free •Grain-Free •Dairy-Free Option •Low-Sugar Option •Paleo

Cinnamon sugar coating on vanilla donuts is an easy donut topping option or a replacement for glazing or frosting your donut (or other baked goods). I use coconut sugar, but feel free to use your sugar of choice. To make the donuts low sugar, replace the honey with ½ teaspoon powdered stevia mixed with ¼ cup (30 g) coconut milk or other milk and reduce the amount of sugar in the topping to ¼ cup. To make this dairy-free, use coconut oil or palm shortening instead of butter or ghee.

FOR DONUTS:

½ cup (52 g) coconut flour

½ teaspoon baking soda

¼ teaspoon salt

¼ teaspoon ground cinnamon

4 large eggs

¼ cup (57 g) unsalted butter, melted, or ghee, coconut oil, or palm shortening

¼ cup (60 ml) coconut milk or other milk

¼ cup (80 g) honey or maple syrup

1 tablespoon (15 ml) vanilla extract

1 teaspoon (5 ml) lemon juice

FOR CINNAMON-SUGAR TOPPING:

½ cup (60 g) coconut sugar

2 tablespoons (14 g) ground cinnamon

¼ cup (57 g) unsalted butter (or coconut oil or palm shortening)

1. Preheat your oven to 350°F (180°C, or gas mark 4).

2. Grease your donut pan or follow the directions for your donut maker.

3. To make the donuts: Place the coconut flour, baking soda, salt, and cinnamon in a bowl and blend well.

4. Add the eggs, butter, milk, honey, vanilla, and lemon juice to a mixing bowl and blend well.

5. Add the dry mix to the wet mix and blend well using a handheld or stand mixer. Let the batter stand for a few minutes and mix once more.

6. Fill the donut pan or maker with batter so it reaches the top of the donut well. To make it easy to fill the donut pan, place the batter in a resealable plastic bag, cut a small piece from one corner, and pipe the batter into the donut wells.

7. Bake the donuts for 15 minutes for regular-size donuts, or until a toothpick inserted in the center of the donut comes out clean.

8. Cool the donuts before dipping them in the topping.

9. To make the topping: Mix the coconut sugar and cinnamon together and place the mixture on a plate. Melt the butter and place in a bowl or on a plate.

10. Dip the top of the donuts in the butter and then in the cinnamon sugar mixture.

11. Store in a sealed container at room temperature for a few days, in the refrigerator for a few weeks, or in the freezer for a few months.

Yield: 8 donuts or 24 mini-donuts

Glazed Coconut Donuts

•Gluten-Free   •Grain-Free   •Dairy-Free Option   •Paleo   •Nut-Free

Chocolate and toasted coconut make a great topping for this cake-like donut. These are a bit denser than the vanilla donuts, and they were one of the first coconut flour recipes that I created, way back when I started Comfy Belly. You can dress these up in a number of ways or just eat them straight up. Or make them as cupcakes, cool, and top with ganache (page 96) and toasted coconut (page 81).

½ cup (52 g) coconut flour

¼ teaspoon salt

¼ teaspoon baking soda

6 large eggs

½ cup (170 g) maple syrup or honey

1 tablespoon (15 ml) vanilla extract

½ cup (114 g) unsalted butter, melted, or coconut oil, palm shortening, or ghee

Chocolate Ganache recipe (page 96)

Toasted coconut recipe (page 81)

1. Preheat your oven to 350°F (180°C, or gas mark 4).

2. Grease your donut pan or follow the directions for your donut maker.

3. In a bowl, whisk together the coconut flour, salt, and baking soda.

4. In a separate bowl, add the eggs, maple syrup, vanilla, and butter and blend together, using a handheld or stand mixer.

5. Add the dry ingredients to the wet ingredients and blend well. Let the batter sit for a few minutes and mix again.

6. Fill the donut wells two-thirds of the way. Follow manufacturer's instructions if you're using a donut maker.

7. Bake the donuts for 15 minutes, or until a toothpick inserted in the center comes out clean.

8. Cool donuts while preparing the ganache and toasted coconut.

9. Place the warm ganache in a wide bowl and the toasted coconut on a plate. Dip each donut in the ganache and then in the toasted coconut. Set each donut aside to cool. You can speed up the cooling by chilling them for 10 minutes.

10. Store in a sealed container at room temperature for a few days, in the refrigerator for a few weeks, or in the freezer for a few months.

Yield: 8 donuts

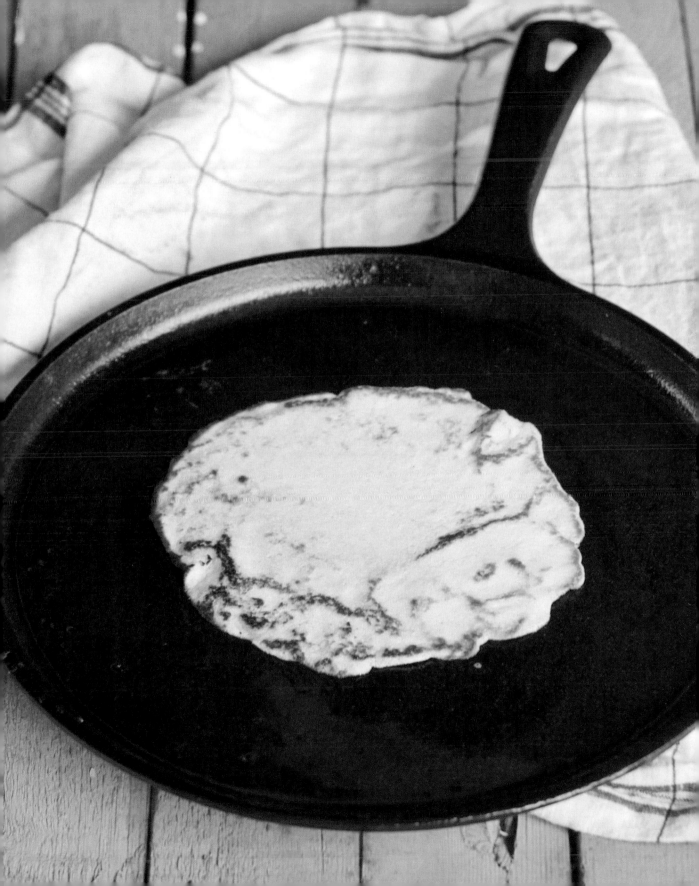

Crêpes

•Gluten-Free •Grain-Free •Dairy-Free Option •Low-Sugar •Paleo •Nut-Free

A crêpe is a light, thin pancake that is filled with a few sweet or savory ingredients. Some popular sweet fillings include jam, fruit, nut butter, and chocolate. For savory fillings, just think of your favorite stir-fry mixture, or any other savory filling that likes a bit of a wrapping around it. Also feel free to add some pepper or other spices that go well with your filling to the savory batter. For a sweet crêpe filling, see the Berry Yogurt Crêpes (page 75). For a savory crêpe filling, see the Mushroom-Feta Spinach Crêpes (page 76).

FOR SWEET CRÊPES:

2 large eggs

2 tablespoons (28 g) unsalted butter, melted, or ghee or coconut oil, plus more for the skillet

1 teaspoon (7 g) honey or maple syrup

⅓ cup (90 ml) coconut milk or other milk

2 tablespoons (13 g) coconut flour

⅛ teaspoon salt

FOR SAVORY CRÊPES:

2 eggs

2 tablespoons (28 g) unsalted butter, melted, or ghee or coconut oil, plus more for the skillet

⅓ cup (90 ml) coconut milk or other milk

2 tablespoons (13 g) coconut flour

⅛ teaspoon salt

1. Whisk together the eggs, 2 tablespoons butter, honey (omit for savory crêpes), and milk.

2. Add the coconut flour and salt and whisk until well blended. Let the batter sit for a few minutes and mix once more.

3. Warm a skillet over medium heat and add about 1 tablespoon (15 ml) oil. Pour about 2 tablespoons (about 22 g) batter into the skillet to make a 4 to 5-inch (10 to 13 cm) crêpe. Tilt the pan to allow the batter to spread across skillet in the shape of a circle.

4. Cook for a few minutes, until the edges and bottom are starting to brown and you can easily slip a spatula underneath; flip the crêpe over. Cook another minute or so, or until it is slightly browned.

5. Transfer the cooked crêpe onto a plate and repeat with the rest of the batter. Place wax paper, parchment paper, or paper towels between the crêpes on the plate to keep them from sticking together.

6. Serve warm. Store in a sealed container in the refrigerator for a week or in the freezer for a month.

Yield: 4 to 6 crêpes

Berry Yogurt Crêpes

•Gluten-Free   •Grain-Free   •Dairy-Free Option   •Paleo   •Nut-Free

Here's a quick recipe for adding simmered berries and yogurt to the sweet crêpes. Of course you can add fresh berries as well, but I favor the simmered berries because they are almost like a fresh jam. In a pinch you can use jam and yogurt.

To make this dairy-free, use dairy-free yogurt and make the dairy-free version of the sweet crêpes by replacing the butter with coconut oil, palm shortening, or another dairy-free fat.

4 Sweet Crêpes (page 73)

1 cup (230 g) yogurt

1 cup (120 g) berry filling

1. Lay the crêpes flat and place about ¼ cup (60 g) yogurt and ¼ cup berry filling on the center of each crêpe.

2. Fold each crêpe closed. The yogurt and berries should be able to keep them closed.

3. Serve warm or room temperature.

Yield: 4 crêpes

BERRY FILLING

A little simmering and you have a sweet little pot of berries you can add to yogurt, ice cream, Banana Porridge (page 129), or freeze for a later time.

1 cup (150 g) fresh blueberries, raspberries, blackberries, or other berries

1 tablespoon (15 ml) lemon juice

2 tablespoons (40 g) honey or maple syrup

Pinch salt (less than ⅛ teaspoon)

1. Add all the ingredients to a saucepan and simmer for 10 minutes, stirring occasionally.

2. Cool and serve. Store in the refrigerator for a week or in the freezer for a few months.

Yield: 1 cup (120 g)

Mushroom-Feta Spinach Crêpes

•Gluten-Free •Grain-Free •Low-Sugar •Nut-Free

Skillet scrambles and quick stir-fried mixes go well in crêpes. You can make the crêpes ahead of time and store them sealed in the refrigerator until you're ready to whip up a scramble. Here's one of my favorite skillet scrambles that makes a great meal. Serve it with Pico de Gallo (page 143) or Roasted Cherry Tomatoes (page 152).

2 tablespoons (30 ml) ghee, coconut oil, or other oil

½ cup (30 g) chopped cremini or other kind of mushrooms

5 ounces (142 g) fresh spinach leaves, chopped

½ cup (56 g) chopped scallions

4½ ounces (127 g) feta cheese

1 large egg

4 Savory Crêpes (page 73)

1. Warm a skillet on medium-high heat and add the ghee. Add the mushrooms to the skillet and cook, stirring occasionally, for 5 minutes, or until they begin to soften and brown.

2. Lower the heat to medium and add the spinach and scallions. Cook for 5 minutes, stirring occasionally.

3. Turn off the heat and add the egg and feta cheese. Blend well.

4. Fill each crêpe with some scramble and serve warm.

Yield: 4 servings

CHAPTER 4

CAKES AND CUPCAKES

⋈

From traditional vanilla and chocolate layer cakes to moist and flavorful red velvet cupcakes and classic coconut cake, you'll be amazed at how great coconut flour is for gluten-free and grain-free cakes and cupcakes. To top them off, there's a variety of frostings to choose from, including dairy-free options. So much delight, in just one chapter!

Yellow Cake

•Gluten-Free •Grain-Free •Dairy-Free Option •Low-Sugar Option •Paleo •Nut-Free

I use this yellow cake for birthday and other cakes, and it works well with all kinds of toppings, frostings, and fillings, between the layers and on top. One of my favorite variations is to whip up some cream, layer with 2 or 3 cakes, and add strawberries on top and in between layers, kind of like a strawberry shortcake.

This recipe makes one layer cake, so double it for two layers. You can use either an 8-inch (20 cm) or 9-inch (23 cm) springform or round baking pan.

To make this low-sugar, replace ¼ cup (80 g) of the maple syrup with ½ teaspoon powdered stevia plus ¼ cup (60 ml) coconut milk or other milk. To make it dairy-free, use coconut oil or palm shortening in place of the butter or ghee.

½ cup (52 g) coconut flour

¼ teaspoon baking soda

¼ teaspoon salt

4 large eggs

⅓ cup (76 g) unsalted butter, melted, or coconut oil, ghee, olive oil, or cooking oil

½ cup (170 g) honey or maple syrup

1 tablespoon (15 ml) vanilla extract

2 tablespoons (28 ml) coconut milk or other milk

1. Preheat your oven to 350°F (180°C, or gas mark 4).

2. Prepare one 8-inch (20 cm) or 9-inch (23 cm) round cake pan by greasing the bottom and sides and placing a circle of parchment paper on the bottom.

3. Add the coconut flour, baking soda, and salt to a large mixing bowl and blend well.

4. Add the eggs, butter, honey, vanilla, and coconut milk to the dry ingredients and use a handheld or stand mixer to blend well.

5. Pour the batter into the baking pan and bake for 20 minutes, or until a toothpick inserted in the center of the cake comes out clean.

6. Cool completely before frosting, filling, and layering.

Yield: 1 one-layer cake

Coconut Cake

•Gluten-Free •Grain-Free •Dairy-Free Option •Paleo •Nut-Free

This two-layer coconut cake recipe uses coconut flour and toasted coconut to bring out true coconut flavor in a tender, moist cake. While most of my coconut flour baked goods don't taste like coconut, this one purposely screams of coconut, in a good way.

This recipe makes two layers; you can use two 8-inch (20 cm) or 9-inch (23 cm) spring-form or round cake pans. You can also divide the recipe in half to make just one layer. Frost it with Coconut Whipped Cream (page 100) or Maple Whipped Cream (page 100), and sprinkle toasted coconut flakes on top (see sidebar).

1 cup (104 g) coconut flour

½ teaspoon salt

½ teaspoon baking soda

½ cup (32 g) unsweetened shredded coconut, toasted (see sidebar)

⅔ cup (150 g) unsalted butter, melted, or coconut oil, palm shortening, or ghee

¼ cup (60 ml) coconut milk or other milk

1 cup (315 g) honey or maple syrup

2 tablespoons (28 ml) vanilla extract

8 large eggs

1. Preheat your oven to 325°F (170°C, or gas mark 3).

2. Grease the bottom and sides of two 8-inch (20 cm) or 9-inch (23 cm) round cake pans and place a circle of parchment paper on the bottom of each pan.

3. Place the coconut flour, salt, and baking soda, and shredded coconut in the bowl of a stand mixer with a paddle attachment or use a large mixing bowl with a handheld mixer, and mix until well blended.

4. Add the butter, coconut milk, honey, vanilla, and eggs to the dry mixture and mix again until the batter is smooth. Let it sit for a few minutes and mix once more.

5. Pour the batter evenly between the two prepared baking pans and bake for 30 minutes, or until a toothpick inserted in the center of the cakes comes out clean.

6. Cool the cakes completely before frosting.

Yield: 1 double-layer cake, or 8 to 12 servings

TOASTED COCONUT

A nice final touch for this cake is to sprinkle toasted shredded or flaked coconut on top of the frosted cake.

½ cup (32 g) unsweetened shredded or flaked coconut

For the oven method: Preheat your oven to 300°F (150°C, or gas mark 2). Spread the coconut across a baking sheet and bake for a few minutes or until they start to turn golden.

For the skillet method: Place the coconut flakes or shredded coconut in a skillet over medium heat, and toast, stirring constantly, for a few minutes, until it begins to turn golden.

Chocolate Layer Cake

•Gluten-Free   •Grain-Free   •Dairy-Free   •Paleo   •Nut-Free

If you're a chocolate lover (as I am), you'll want to frost this cake with a rich chocolate frosting. If you're not, the whipped cream or coconut cream frostings are a nice white balance to the chocolate darkness of this cake—it's a bit darker than the Chocolate Zucchini Cake (page 45). This is a light, easy cake to make, and a good option that calls for basic ingredients.

For a full-on chocolate experience, frost it with the Simple Chocolate Frosting (page 98) or the Chocolate Buttercream Frosting (page 98). Another option is to pour the Chocolate Ganache (page 96) on top of the cooled layer of cake and then top with raspberries.

This recipe makes one layer, so just double the recipe for a two-layer cake.

¼ cup (26 g) coconut flour

¼ cup (20 g) unsweetened cocoa

¼ teaspoon salt

¼ teaspoon of baking soda

3 large eggs

½ cup (170 g) maple syrup or honey

2 tablespoons (28 ml) coconut milk or other milk

1. Preheat your oven to 350°F (180°C, or gas mark 4)

2. Prepare an 8-inch (20 cm) or 9-inch (23 cm) round cake pan by greasing it and placing a parchment paper circle on the bottom of each pan.

3. Place the coconut flour, cocoa, salt, and baking soda in a large bowl and blend well.

4. Add the eggs, maple syrup, and milk to the dry ingredients and mix with a handheld or stand mixer until well blended. Let the batter sit for a few minutes and mix once more. This batter is somewhat thin, so don't be alarmed if it doesn't thicken like some of the other cake batters.

5. Pour the batter into the cake pans. Bake for about 20 minutes, or until a toothpick inserted in the center of the cake comes out clean.

6. Cool and frost.

Yield: 1 two-layer cake, or 8 to 12 servings

Carrot Cake

•Gluten-Free   •Grain-Free   •Dairy-Free Option   •Low-Sugar Option   •Paleo   •Nut-Free

Medjool dates are on the lower side of the glycemic index scale, so they won't give you as large a spike in blood sugar as maple syrup or honey. To soften the dates so they're easier to chop, soak them in hot water for 10 minutes or so, and then drain and pat them dry. Carrot cake does tend to be sweet in part because of the carrots, so if you'd like to reduce the sweetener a bit, replace ¼ cup (80 g) of the maple syrup with ½ teaspoon stevia plus ¼ cup (60 ml) coconut milk or other dairy-free milk.

5½ ounces (160 g) Medjool dates (about 8 dates), pitted and finely chopped or pulsed in a food processor

½ cup (114 g) unsalted butter (or coconut oil, ghee, or palm shortening), melted

½ cup (120 ml) coconut milk or other milk

8 large eggs

4 cups (280 g) shredded or grated raw carrots, loosely packed (about 4 large carrots)

1 tablespoon (15 ml) vanilla extract

½ cup (170 g) maple syrup or honey

¾ cup (78 g) coconut flour

2 teaspoons (5 g) ground cinnamon

1 teaspoon (2.2 g) ground nutmeg

½ teaspoon ground cloves

1 teaspoon (4.6 g) baking soda

1 teaspoon (6 g) salt

½ cup (56 g) chopped nuts (optional)

Maple Cream Cheese Frosting (page 101), Maple Cream Frosting (page 101), or Vanilla Cream Frosting (page 99)

1. Preheat your oven to 350°F (180°C, or gas mark 4).

2. Prepare two 8-inch (20 cm) or 9-inch (23 cm) round cake pans by greasing them and placing parchment paper cut into circles on the bottom of each pan.

3. Add the dates, butter, milk, eggs, carrots, vanilla, and maple syrup to a mixing bowl and blend well with a mixer or by hand.

4. In a separate bowl, whisk together flour, cinnamon, nutmeg, cloves, baking soda, salt, and nuts. Add the dry mixture to the wet mixture and blend well.

5. Divide the batter equally between the two cake pans and bake for 35 to 40 minutes, or until a toothpick inserted in the middle of each cake comes out clean.

6. Cool cakes completely and then frost. Store in the refrigerator for a week or so.

Yield: 1 two-layer cake, or 8 to 12 servings

Cinnamon Streusel Cake (or Loaf)

•Gluten-Free   •Grain-Free   •Dairy-Free Option   •Paleo   •Nut-Free

This recipe is based on the cinnamon bun muffin recipe with a bit of shifting in the amount of sweetener and the addition of coconut milk. Sometimes I just want one loaf to slice up and store as a whole and this recipe is just that.

As for the baking pan size, you have some flexibility here. You can use either a 7.5 × 3.5 × 2.25-inch (19 × 9 × 7 cm) loaf pan or an 8 × 8 × 2-inch (20 × 20 × 5 cm) square cake pan.

Make this dairy-free by replacing the yogurt with coconut milk or other dairy-free milk. For the streusel topping, you can use coconut sugar or maple sugar in place of the maple syrup or honey.

FOR THE LOAF:

½ cup (52 g) coconut flour

¼ teaspoon baking soda

¼ teaspoon salt

4 large eggs

⅓ cup (77 g) yogurt or dairy-free milk

⅓ cup (105 g) honey or maple syrup

2 tablespoons (28 ml) coconut milk or other milk

FOR THE STREUSEL TOPPING:

2 tablespoons (14 g) ground cinnamon

¼ cup (80 g) honey or maple syrup, or other sweetener

2 tablespoons (28 g) unsalted butter, ghee, or coconut oil melted

⅓ cup (37 g) chopped walnuts or pecans (optional)

1. Preheat oven to 350°F (180°C, or gas mark 4).

2. Grease the baking pan (see above) well, or line the bottom with parchment paper and grease the sides; dust with a small amount of coconut flour.

3. To make the loaf: Whisk the flour, baking soda, and salt together in a bowl.

4. Add the eggs, yogurt, honey, and coconut milk to the flour mixture and blend well, using a mixer or a food processor. Let the batter sit for a few minutes.

5. To make the cinnamon topping: Place the cinnamon, honey, butter, and walnuts in a small bowl and mix together with a fork or whisk.

6. Scoop the batter into the baking pan and then pour the topping over the batter. Use a fork to swirl the topping around the batter.

7. Bake the loaf for 40 minutes, or until a toothpick inserted in the center comes out clean.

8. Cool and slice.

Yield: 1 loaf

Vanilla Cupcakes

•Gluten-Free   •Grain-Free   •Dairy-Free Option   •Low-Sugar Option   •Paleo   •Nut-Free

Just in case you don't like chocolate or need a change, here's a deliciously simple vanilla cupcake recipe. I've used this recipe as a base for several others, and it can withstand a number of variations and additions. You can make this low-sugar by replacing ¼ cup of honey or maple syrup with ¼ cup (60 ml) coconut milk and ½ teaspoon powdered stevia. To make it dairy-free, use coconut oil or olive oil instead of butter or ghee.

½ cup (52 g) coconut flour

¼ teaspoon baking soda

¼ teaspoon salt

4 large eggs

⅓ cup (76 g) unsalted butter, melted, or coconut oil, ghee, olive oil, or cooking oil

½ cup (170 g) honey or maple syrup

1 tablespoon (15 ml) vanilla extract

2 tablespoons (28 ml) coconut milk or other milk

1. Preheat your oven to 350°F (180°C, or gas mark 4).

2. Prepare a cupcake pan with cupcake liners.

3. Add the coconut flour, baking soda, and salt to a bowl and blend well.

4. In a separate bowl, whisk together the eggs, butter, honey, vanilla, and coconut milk. Add this mixture to the dry ingredients and use a handheld or stand mixer to blend well. Let the batter sit for a few minutes and then mix once more.

5. Fill the cupcake liners about three-quarters of the way with batter and bake for 20 minutes, or until a toothpick inserted in the center of a cupcake comes out clean.

6. Cool and frost. Store the cupcakes, covered, at room temperature for a few days, in the refrigerator for a few weeks, or in the freezer for a few months.

Yield: 8 cupcakes

Red Velvet Cupcakes

•Gluten-Free •Grain-Free •Dairy-Free Option •Paleo •Nut-Free

I use red beet juice to get a rich reddish-brown color for this cupcake, but in a pinch you can use 1 to 2 tablespoons (15 to 28 ml) of natural red food dye. Traditionally, red velvet cupcakes and cake are frosted with cream cheese frosting, so try the Maple Cream Cheese Frosting (page 101) or the Dairy-Free Maple Cream Frosting (page 101). To make this dairy-free, substitute coconut milk or use a dairy-free yogurt for the yogurt.

½ cup (52 g) coconut flour

2 tablespoons (11 g) unsweetened cocoa

½ teaspoon salt

¼ teaspoon baking soda

4 large eggs

2 tablespoons (28 ml) olive oil or other oil

½ cup (170 g) maple syrup or honey

1 tablespoon (15 g) plain yogurt or cultured sour cream

1 teaspoon (5 ml) vanilla extract

2 tablespoons (28 ml) lemon juice

2 tablespoons (28 ml) beet juice (about 1 medium red beet; see sidebar)

Frosting of your choice (see headnote)

1. Preheat your oven to 350°F (180°C, or gas mark 4).

2. Line a cupcake pan with cupcake liners or use silicon cupcake liners. Even if you're using parchment paper liners I suggest greasing the liners for this recipe to prevent the cupcakes from sticking.

3. Whisk the coconut flour, cocoa, salt, and baking soda together in a bowl.

4. Whisk the eggs, oil, maple syrup, yogurt, vanilla, and lemon juice and then add the mixture to the dry ingredients and mix, using a handheld or stand mixer. Add the beet juice and mix again. Let the batter sit for a few minutes and mix once more.

5. Fill the cupcake liners three-quarters of the way with batter. Tap the pan gently to even out the batter.

6. Bake for 20 minutes, or until a toothpick inserted in the center comes out clean.

7. Cool and frost. Store, covered, at room temperature for a few days, in the refrigerator for a few weeks, or in the freezer for a few months.

Yield: 8 cupcakes

HOW TO MAKE BEET JUICE

In a juicer: Prepare the beets by cleaning off any soil and debris, trim and peel any roots and stems, and peel the outer skin. Chop the beets into pieces, and add them to your juicer to extract the juice.

In a blender: Clean, peel, and chop the beets as noted in the juicer technique. Add the beets to a blender with just enough water to get the blender moving and blend until smooth. Pour the blended beets over a mesh strainer covering a bowl. Use a spatula to press down on the beets and extract the juice.

Chocolate Cloud Cupcakes

•Gluten-Free •Grain-Free •Dairy-Free •Paleo

Perfect for an everyday muffin or cupcake, these light fluffy chocolate cupcakes are not too sweet and go exceptionally well with the Whipped Chocolate Frosting (page 96). We also like to add chocolate chips to them. To prevent them from sinking to the bottom of the thin batter, use only about ½ cup (84 g) chocolate chips and add a few to each cupcake after you've filled the cupcake liner. I sprinkle them across each cupcake and then shuffle the cupcake pan back and forth to allow the chips to sink a bit into the batter.

¼ cup (26 g) coconut flour

¼ cup (20 g) unsweetened cocoa

¼ teaspoon salt

¼ teaspoon of baking soda

3 large eggs

½ cup (170 g) maple syrup or honey

2 tablespoons (28 ml) coconut milk or other milk

1. Preheat your oven to 350°F (180°C, or gas mark 4).

2. Prepare a cupcake pan with parchment cupcake liners.

3. Add the coconut flour, cocoa, salt, and baking soda to a bowl and blend well.

4. Whisk the eggs, maple syrup, and milk together and then add the mixture to the dry ingredients and mix, using a handheld or stand mixer until well blended. Let the batter sit for a few minutes and mix once more. This batter is somewhat thin, so don't be alarmed if it doesn't thicken like some other muffin and cupcake batters.

5. Fill each cupcake liner halfway with batter. Bake for about 15 minutes, or until a toothpick inserted in the center of a cupcake comes out clean.

6. Cool and frost. Store in a sealed container at room temperature for a few days, in the refrigerator for a few weeks, or in the freezer for a few months.

Yield: 8 cupcakes

Almond Cake

•Gluten-Free   •Grain-Free   •Dairy-Free Option   •Paleo

I like to use this recipe for layer cakes and other kinds of cakes when using nuts are not an issue and I want a buttery-rich flavor. It's a bit denser than the Yellow Cake (page 79) because almond flour is denser than coconut flour. Finely ground blanched almonds lend great flavor and texture to cakes and muffins, and almond flour is high in protein like coconut flour so the two flours are complementary in health benefits as well as flavor and texture.

This recipe makes one layer, so double the ingredients for a two-layer cake and mix well. To make this recipe dairy-free, use coconut oil or palm shortening in place of butter.

½ cup (48 g) blanched almond flour

¼ cup (26 g) coconut flour

¼ teaspoon salt

¼ teaspoon baking soda

3 eggs

¼ cup (57 g) unsalted butter, melted, or coconut oil, palm shortening, ghee, or other oil

3 tablespoons (60 g) honey or maple syrup

½ cup (120 ml) coconut milk or other milk

1 teaspoon (5 ml) vanilla extract

1. Preheat your oven to 325°F (170°C, or gas mark 3).

2. Line the bottom of an 8-inch (20 cm) round cake pan with a parchment paper circle or grease the pan well.

3. Place the almond and coconut flours, salt, and baking soda in a mixing bowl and stir until well blended.

4. Add the eggs, butter, honey, milk, and vanilla to the dry mixture and blend well using a handheld or stand mixer.

5. Pour the batter into the prepared pan and bake for 20 minutes, or until a toothpick inserted in the center of the cake comes out clean.

6. Let the cake cool for an hour if you plan to frost it. Gently run a knife around the outside edge of the cake to make it easy to remove from the pan.

Yield: 1 one-layer cake

Carrot Cupcakes

•Gluten-Free   •Grain-Free   •Dairy-Free Option   •Low-Sugar Option   •Paleo   •Nut-Free

This is a light, sweet carrot-packed cupcake that you'll feel good about eating. After all, it's loaded with carrots, natural sweetener, and spices.

This cupcake is sweet partly because of the carrots. To reduce the amount of sweetness, substitute ½ teaspoon powdered stevia plus ¼ cup (60 ml) coconut milk or other milk for the maple syrup or honey. To make this dairy-free, use coconut oil or palm shortening in place of butter or ghee.

¼ cup (57 g) unsalted butter, melted, or ghee, oil, or coconut oil

¼ cup (60 ml) coconut milk or other milk

4 large eggs

2 cups (140 g) shredded or grated raw carrots, loosely packed, (about 4 large carrots)

¼ cup (80 g) maple syrup or honey

2 teaspoons (28 ml) vanilla extract

¼ cup plus 2 tablespoons (39 g) coconut flour

1 teaspoon (2 g) ground cinnamon

½ teaspoon ground nutmeg

¼ teaspoon ground cloves

½ teaspoon of baking soda

½ teaspoon of salt

Maple Cream Cheese Frosting (page 101) or Vanilla Frosting (page 99)

1. Preheat your oven to 350°F (180°C, or gas mark 4).

2. Prepare a cupcake pan with cupcake liners.

3. Add the butter, milk, eggs, carrots, maple syrup, and vanilla to a mixing bowl and blend well. I use a mixer for this step, but you can mix by hand as well.

4. In a separate bowl, whisk together the coconut flour, cinnamon, nutmeg, cloves, baking soda, and salt.

5. Add the dry mixture to the wet mixture and blend well. Let the batter sit for a few minutes and blend once more.

6. Fill the cupcake liners three-quarters full and bake for 20 minutes, or until a toothpick inserted in the center of a cupcake comes out clean.

7. Cool cakes completely and then frost. Store the frosted cupcakes in the refrigerator for a week or so.

Yield: 8 cupcakes

Chocolate Ganache and Whipped Chocolate Frosting

•Gluten-Free   •Grain-Free   •Nut-Free   •Egg-Free

Whipping cream with sweetened chocolate results in a light, creamy chocolate frosting that is perfect for cupcakes and cakes. This frosting works well for the Chocolate Cloud Cupcakes (page 93), but it goes just as well on just about any cupcake or cake. Or eat it straight up with a spoon, as I've been known to do.

There are actually two recipes here: chocolate ganache and whipped chocolate frosting. You'll have ganache after you've melted the chocolate in the heavy cream. At this point you can cool the mixture and then spread it across cakes or cupcakes (it's great as a frosting for the Chocolate Layer Cake on page 83), or take it to the next level and whip it, and you'll have a light, creamy chocolate frosting that resembles chocolate buttercream frosting.

1 cup (235 ml) heavy cream

1½ cups (252 g) dark chocolate chips or chopped dark chocolate

Pinch salt (less than ⅛ teaspoon)

1. Place the cream in a saucepan, bring to a soft boil, and then turn off the heat.

2. Add the chocolate to the cream and stir to dissolve.

3. Cool to room temperature. The longer it cools, the thicker it will get. You can chill it a few minutes in the refrigerator to speed up the cooling process. You can then use it as a ganache or make whipped frosting.

4. To use it as ganache, chill it in the refrigerator until it's thick enough to pour or to spread as frosting.

5. To make the whipped chocolate frosting, use a whisk or handheld or stand mixer to whip the mixture for a few minutes until it becomes light and creamy. It can be stored in a sealed container in the refrigerator for a few days. Frost the whipped chocolate when it is at room temperature.

Yield: About 2 cups (490 g)

MAKE YOUR OWN PASTRY BAG

If you don't have a pastry bag, you can convert a Ziploc bag into one. Simply place the bag halfway into a cup and scoop the frosting into the bag. Lift the bag out of the cup, seal, and guide the frosting toward the bottom of one corner of the bag. Snip off a tiny piece of the corner and start piping!

Note that if you have a pastry tip, you can cut a small hole in one corner of the bag first, slip the pastry tip inside the hole, then fill with frosting and pipe.

Dairy-Free Chocolate Ganache

•Gluten-Free   •Grain-Free   •Dairy-Free   •Paleo   •Nut-Free   •Egg-Free

Here's a simple ganache recipe that can be made in one saucepan in 5 minutes. Yes, it's that simple. The coconut oil or palm shortening makes it dairy-free, but you can use butter if dairy isn't an issue. If you're using this for a layer cake, you'll want to double the recipe to cover both layers.

¼ cup (60 ml) coconut oil or palm shortening

¼ cup (20 g) unsweetened cocoa powder

2 tablespoons (40 g) maple syrup or honey

½ teaspoon vanilla

Pinch salt (less than ⅛ teaspoon)

1. Melt the coconut oil in a small saucepan over a low heat. It won't take long for the oil to melt because it has a low melting point, which is why it's sometimes a liquid in your pantry during hot summer days.

2. Turn the heat off and stir in the cocoa powder, maple syrup, vanilla, and salt.

3. Let the ganache cool to room temperature or to speed things up, place the saucepan in the refrigerator for about 5 minutes.

4. Spoon or drizzle the ganache over cupcakes, cakes, muffins, and cookies. Let it cool at room temperature for 5 minutes or so, or refrigerate until ready to devour.

5. You can store the ganache in a sealed container in the refrigerator for a few weeks. Reheat on a low heat to use it again.

Yield: About ½ cup (134 g)

Chocolate Buttercream Frosting

•Gluten-Free   •Grain-Free   •Nut-Free   •Egg-Free

This buttercream frosting uses maple syrup for sweetener, which is a healthier alternative to powdered sugar, or you can also use honey if you prefer. To make this dairy-free, substitute palm shortening or coconut oil for the butter.

½ cup (114 g) unsalted butter, softened

2 tablespoons (40 g) maple syrup or honey

½ cup (40 g) unsweetened cocoa

1 teaspoon (5 ml) vanilla extract

Pinch salt

1. Place the butter in a mixing bowl and mix using a handheld or stand mixer until the butter begins to get creamy.

2. Add the maple syrup, cocoa, vanilla, and salt and mix for a few minutes or until the frosting is creamy.

3. Frost at room temperature.

Yield: About ¾ cup (235 g)

Simple Chocolate Frosting

•Gluten-Free   •Grain-Free   •Dairy-Free Option   •Paleo
•Nut-Free   •Egg-Free

This is possibly one of the easiest frostings to make when you have some sweetened chocolate chips or a chocolate bar on hand. The better the quality and flavor of your chocolate, the better the frosting will be. I use semisweet chocolate chips (see Resources, page 154) when I make these, but you can use any kind of chocolate.

1 cup (168 g) chocolate chips or chopped chocolate

⅓ cup (76 g) unsalted butter, or coconut oil, palm shortening, or ghee

1 teaspoon (5 ml) vanilla extract

Pinch salt (less than ⅛ teaspoon)

1. Place about 1 cup (235 ml) of water in a saucepan, set the saucepan on a medium-low heat, and bring the water to a simmer. Place a glass bowl on top of the saucepan, without letting the bottom of the bowl touch the water, and add the chocolate chips and butter. Slowly melt the chocolate and butter, stirring occasionally.

2. When the chocolate is just about to finish melting, turn off the heat, and stir until creamy. Add the vanilla and salt and stir to blend well.

3. Cool the frosting at room temperature for 30 minutes or so, or chill in the refrigerator for about 5 minutes to speed up the cooling process.

4. Store in a sealed container in the refrigerator for a few weeks.

Yield: About 1¼ cups (245 g)

Vanilla Cream Frosting

•Gluten-Free •Grain-Free •Dairy-Free •Paleo
•Egg-Free

This frosting can be used on muffins, cakes, or cupcakes. It does require a bit of planning—you'll need about 3 hours to soak the cashews until they are soft enough to yield a creamy frosting. If you don't have dates, you can use 1 to 2 tablespoons (20 to 40 g) of maple syrup, honey, or other sweetener.

1 cup (110 g) raw cashews, soaked in water for 3 hours

2 tablespoons (30 ml) apple juice

1½ ounces (40 g) Medjool dates (about 2 dates), pitted

1 tablespoon (15 ml) vanilla extract, or the seeds of 1 vanilla bean

Pinch salt (up to ⅛ teaspoon)

1. Place all the ingredients in a high-speed blender or food processor and blend until creamy.

2. Store in a sealed container in the refrigerator for a week or so.

Yield: About 2 cups (290 g)

Dairy-Free Vanilla Frosting

•Gluten-Free •Grain-Free •Dairy-Free •Paleo
•Nut-Free •Egg-Free

Palm shortening makes up the base of this dairy-free vanilla frosting. See Resources, page 154, for available brands.

1½ cups (250 g) palm shortening

1 cup (315 g) honey or maple syrup

1 tablespoon (15 ml) coconut milk or other milk

1 tablespoon (15 ml) vanilla extract

1. Using a handheld or stand mixer, blend the shortening on a slow speed until it becomes creamy.

2. Add the honey, milk, and vanilla extract and continue mixing until the frosting is well blended and creamy. Adjust the sweetener to suit your taste.

3. Frost a cake or cupcakes at room temperature. Store frosting in a sealed container in the refrigerator for a few weeks.

Yield: About 1½ cups (about 320 g)

Maple Whipped Cream

•Gluten-Free •Grain-Free •Low- Sugar Option
•Nut-Free •Egg-Free

Maple syrup is the sweetener for this recipe; however, feel free to use another liquid or crystal sweetener to create whipped cream. This recipe makes enough to frost 8 cupcakes, so if you want to use it to frost a two-layer cake, double the recipe. To make this low sugar, use ⅛ teaspoon of powdered stevia, or to taste.

1 cup (235 ml) heavy cream

1 to 2 tablespoons (20 to 40 g) maple syrup, or to taste

Add the cream and maple syrup to a bowl or mixing bowl and use a whisk attachment on a handheld or stand mixer to whip the cream until it becomes light and the peaks are stiff. This will take a few minutes.

Yield: About 2 cups (268 g)

Coconut Whipped Cream

•Gluten-Free •Grain-Free •Dairy-Free •Low-Sugar
•Paleo •Nut-Free •Egg-Free

Coconut whipped cream can be used as a substitute for dairy-based cream in many recipes. The trick to getting coconut cream from coconut milk is to refrigerate the full-fat coconut milk (24 hours is best) so that the cream separates out while chilling. Then you skim the cream off the top. Another option is to purchase coconut cream (see Resources, page 154). My favorite brand of coconut milk and coconut cream is Aroy-D because it has no additives.

2 pints (945 ml) coconut milk

2 teaspoons (14 g) honey or maple syrup, or to taste

1 teaspoon (10 ml) vanilla extract

1. Place the coconut milk in the refrigerator for 24 hours.

2. Gently skim the cream off the top of the coconut milk, being careful not to take any liquid below it.

3. Place the cream in a mixing bowl and whip it using a handheld or stand mixer. As it begins to get lighter, drizzle honey or maple syrup into the whipped coconut and keep whipping until it is creamy and light.

4. Store, covered, in the refrigerator for a few days and rewhip as necessary.

Yield: 1 cup (470 g)

Maple Cream Cheese Frosting

•Gluten-Free •Grain-Free •Nut-Free •Egg-Free

This creamy, sweet and slightly tangy frosting is easy to make and store in the refrigerator until you're ready to use it. It goes well with the Carrot Cake (page 85) and the Morning Glory Muffins (page 65), and can also be used to frost a two-layer cake. Look for a cream cheese that doesn't have additives, and if you can't find one, use *fromage blanc* (farmer's cheese) or dripped (Greek) yogurt for this recipe.

1 pound (455 g) cream cheese or fromage blanc

½ cup (170 g) maple syrup

Combine all the ingredients in a bowl and whisk until fully blended.

Yield: About 1½ cups (625 g)

Dairy-Free Maple Cream Frosting

•Gluten-Free •Grain-Free •Dairy-Free •Paleo •Egg-Free

This frosting can be used on just about any muffin, cake, or cupcake. It does require a bit of planning—you'll need about 3 hours to soak the cashews until they are soft enough to yield a creamy frosting. If you don't have dates, you can use 1 to 2 tablespoons (20 to 40 g) of maple syrup, honey, or other sweetener.

1 cup (110 g) raw cashews, soaked in water for 3 hours

2 tablespoons (30 ml) apple juice

2 teaspoons (10 ml) lemon juice

1½ ounces (40 g) Medjool dates (about 2 dates), pitted

2 teaspoons (10 ml) vanilla extract

Pinch salt (up to ⅛ teaspoon)

1. Place all the ingredients in a high-speed blender or food processor and blend until creamy.
2. Store in a sealed container in the refrigerator for a week or so.

Yield: About 2 cups (300 g)

CHAPTER 5

BROWNIES, COOKIES, AND BARS

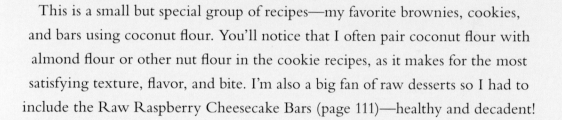

This is a small but special group of recipes—my favorite brownies, cookies, and bars using coconut flour. You'll notice that I often pair coconut flour with almond flour or other nut flour in the cookie recipes, as it makes for the most satisfying texture, flavor, and bite. I'm also a big fan of raw desserts so I had to include the Raw Raspberry Cheesecake Bars (page 111)—healthy and decadent!

Espresso Brownies

•Gluten-Free •Grain-Free •Dairy-Free Option •Paleo •Nut-Free

This chocolate brownie is deep flavored, thanks to the addition of sweetened chocolate, espresso powder, and ganache. If you feel there's more than enough caffeine in the chocolate, you can forgo the espresso in the brownie or the ganache. To make these dairy-free, use palm shortening or coconut oil in place of the butter or ghee.

½ cup (84 g) semisweet chocolate chips or chopped dark chocolate, divided

⅓ cup (76 g) unsalted butter, melted, or ghee, palm shortening, or coconut oil

½ cup (52 g) coconut flour

½ cup (40 g) unsweetened cocoa powder

½ teaspoon espresso powder, or 1 tablespoon (3 g) instant coffee

½ teaspoon salt

6 large eggs

¾ cup (235 g) maple syrup or honey

3 tablespoons (45 ml) coconut milk or other milk

1 teaspoon (5 ml) vanilla extract

Chocolate Ganache (page 96), or dairy-free version (page 97)

ESPRESSO GANACHE

If you want to give your frosting some coffee flavor as well, simply proceed with either the regular (page 96) or dairy-free (page 97) ganache recipe, adding ½ teaspoon espresso powder, or 1 tablespoon (3 g) instant coffee to the other melted ingredients.

1. Preheat your oven to 350°F (180°C, or gas mark 4).

2. Grease an 8 × 8 × 2-inch (20 × 20 × 5 cm) baking pan generously, or line the bottom with parchment paper and grease the sides.

3. Reserve 1 tablespoon (10 g) of the chocolate chips. Bring some water in a saucepan to a simmer and place a glass bowl on top of it, without letting the bowl touch the water. Place the remaining chocolate chips and the butter in the bowl and melt, stirring occasionally. When melted, turn off the heat, add the reserved chocolate chips, and blend until they melt into the mixture.

4. Whisk together the coconut flour, cocoa powder, espresso, and salt in a bowl until they are well blended.

5. In a separate bowl mix together the melted chocolate mixture, eggs, maple syrup, milk, and vanilla until well blended.

6. Add the flour mixture to the egg mixture and blend well, using a mixer or food processor. Let the batter sit for a few minutes and mix once more.

7. Use a spatula to scoop the batter into the baking pan and bake for 25 minutes, or until a toothpick inserted in the middle of the brownies comes out clean. Don't overbake—brownies are always better a bit moister than drier.

8. Cool and cover with ganache, or just eat as is. Store in a sealed container at room temperature for a few days or in the refrigerator for a few weeks.

Yield: 12 brownies

Cake Brownies

•Gluten-Free •Grain-Free •Dairy-Free Option •Paleo •Nut-Free

I've spent quite a bit of kitchen time coming up with a cake brownie that I want to make over and over again because we all know brownies are not a one-time thing. No need to frost this; however, frosting *does* make it that much more decadent. The Simple Chocolate Frosting (page 98) or the Chocolate Ganache (page 96) are both a perfect match. Or go in another direction and add chocolate chips or walnuts to the batter. To make this dairy-free, use coconut oil or palm shortening in place of the butter or ghee.

½ cup (52 g) coconut flour

½ cup (40 g) unsweetened cocoa powder

½ teaspoon salt

½ teaspoon baking soda

5 large eggs

¾ cup (235 g) maple syrup or honey

⅓ cup (76 g) unsalted butter, melted, or ghee, palm shortening, or coconut oil

2 tablespoons (28 ml) coconut milk or other milk

1 teaspoon (5 ml) vanilla extract

1. Preheat your oven to 350°F (180°C, or gas mark 4).

2. Generously grease an 8 × 8 × 2-inch (20 × 20 × 5 cm) baking pan, or line the bottom with parchment paper and grease the sides.

3. Whisk together the coconut flour, cocoa, salt, and baking soda in a large bowl until they are well blended.

4. In a separate bowl mix together the eggs, maple syrup, butter, milk, and vanilla until well blended.

5. Add the cocoa mixture to the egg mixture and blend well, using a mixer or food processor. Let the batter sit for a few minutes and mix once more.

6. Bake for 20 minutes, or until a toothpick inserted in the middle of the brownies comes out clean. Don't overbake—brownies are always better a bit moister than drier.

7. Store in a sealed container at room temperature for a few days or in the refrigerator for a few weeks.

Yield: 12 brownies

Chocolate Chip Cookies

Gluten-Free ▾Grain-Free ▾Dairy-Free Option ▾Paleo ▾Egg-Free Option

Want fresh-baked cookies anytime? Just make the dough and freeze it; then shape them by hand. Or, if you want to bake them now, roll about a tablespoon of dough in your hands, place the ball on the baking mat, and flatten it with your palm to shape the cookie; repeat for each cookie.

I like to use coconut sugar, which is a lower glycemic sweetener than regular granulated sugar, but you can substitute another granulated sugar such as whole cane sugar or maple sugar (see Resources, page 154).

¼ cup (57 g) unsalted butter, softened, or coconut oil, palm shortening, or ghee

¼ cup (30 g) coconut sugar, or whole cane sugar or maple sugar

1 tablespoon (20 g) honey or maple syrup

1 large egg

2 teaspoons (28 ml) vanilla extract

1½ cups (144 g) blanched almond flour

2 tablespoons (13 g) coconut flour

¼ teaspoon baking soda

¼ teaspoon salt

½ cup (84 g) chocolate chips

EGG-FREE AND DAIRY-FREE OPTIONS

To make this egg-free, replace the egg with 1 tablespoon (7 g) flaxseed meal + 3 tablespoons (45 ml) water. Mix, let sit for a minute, then add it to the batter.

To make this dairy-free, use coconut oil or palm shortening in place of the butter or ghee.

1. Add the butter, sugar, honey, egg, and vanilla to a bowl and mix until well blended. A stand or handheld mixer works well. This mixture won't become creamy.

2. Whisk the almond flour, coconut flour, baking soda, and salt together in a separate bowl, then add it to the wet batter and mix well. Stir in the chocolate chips.

3. At this point you can freeze the dough then slice it, or skip ahead and preheat the oven, shape the dough by hand, and bake. To freeze the dough so the cookies are sliceable, scrape the batter out of the bowl and onto a piece of parchment paper. Wrap and roll the dough into a round log. Twist the ends of the paper to push the dough closer together and to close each end.

4. Freeze or chill the dough for at least 30 minutes.

5. Preheat oven to 350°F (180°C, or gas mark 4).

6. Unroll the dough, slice the cookies about ¼ inch (6 mm) thick, and place them on baking sheets lined with parchment paper or on a nonstick baking mat. Space them about ½ inch (13 mm) apart, since they don't spread while baking.

7. Bake for 12 to 15 minutes, or until they are just starting to turn golden.

8. Store the cookie dough tightly sealed in the freezer for several months.

Yield: About 20 cookies

Snickerdoodles

•Gluten-Free   •Grain-Free   •Dairy-Free   •Paleo
•Egg-Free

Snickerdoodles are cinnamon sugar cookies that have a chewy bite to them. The combination of almond flour and coconut flour for this version creates a nice balance of sweetness, spice, and buttery flavor, thanks to the almond flour. These cookies get soft after a day or so, so if you want to regain the crunchy edges, pop them in a warm oven or in a dehydrator for several minutes.

2 cups (192 g) blanched almond flour

2 tablespoons (13 g) coconut flour

¼ teaspoon baking soda

¼ teaspoon salt

3 tablespoons (42 g) unsalted butter, melted, or coconut oil or ghee

⅓ cup (105 g) honey or maple syrup

1 tablespoon (15 ml) vanilla extract

2 tablespoons (14 g) ground cinnamon

2 tablespoons (16 g) coconut sugar, whole cane sugar, or other brown crystallized sugar (or leave it out and just lightly roll in some cinnamon)

1. Preheat oven to 350°F (180°C, or gas mark 4).

2. Whisk together the almond flour, coconut flour, baking soda, and salt in a bowl.

3. In a separate bowl, cream the butter, honey, and vanilla.

4. Add the flour mixture to the butter mixture and blend well. If the batter is a bit soft to handle, chill it for 10 minutes.

5. Line baking sheets with a nonstick surface, Silpat mat, or parchment paper.

6. Blend the ground cinnamon and sugar together in a shallow bowl or plate. Using the palms of your hands, roll a tablespoon or so of dough into a ball. Roll the dough ball in the cinnamon mixture to fully coat. Place the dough balls on the cookie sheet, spaced about an inch (2.5 cm) or so apart, and flatten with the underside of a jar or glass or the palm of your hand.

7. Bake the cookies for 8 to 10 minutes. Cool for at least 10 minutes.

8. Store in a sealed container at room temperature for a few days or in the freezer for a few months.

Yield: 20 cookies

Raw Raspberry Cheesecake Bars

•Gluten-Free   •Grain-Free   •Dairy-Free   •Paleo   •Egg-Free

Raw cheesecake brownies are not baked—the brownie and cheesecake layers are made with nuts and a small amount of coconut flour. You can substitute pecans or other soft nut for the walnuts and use raisins in place of the dates.

To soak the cashews, place them in a bowl with twice the amount of water in volume, making sure all the cashews are covered with water while they soak. Soak for at least 3 hours. I usually leave them to soak overnight on my countertop. When you're ready to use them, rinse them with water, drain them completely, and you're ready to add them to the recipe.

I use a food processor to pulse and blend all the ingredients, but you can also use a high-speed blender. I just find it easier to scoop out the batters from the food processor container.

FOR THE BROWNIE LAYER:

2 cups (240 g) raw walnuts, pecans, macadamia, or other soft nut or seed

1 cup (86 g) unsweetened cacao or cocoa

1 teaspoon (2 g) coconut flour

¼ teaspoon salt

½ teaspoon vanilla extract

2½ cups (320 g) Medjool dates (about 16 dates), pitted

FOR THE CHEESECAKE LAYER:

1½ cups (165 g) raw cashews, soaked in water for at least 3 hours

⅓ cup (80 ml) coconut oil

⅓ cup (80 ml) lemon juice

⅓ cup (105 g) honey or maple syrup

1 teaspoon (5 ml) vanilla extract

1 cup (120 g) raspberries

1. Grease an 8 × 8 × 2-inch (20 × 20 × 5 cm) baking pan with coconut oil.

2. To make the brownie layer: Place the walnuts in a food processor and process until finely ground. Add the cacao, coconut flour, and salt to the walnuts and pulse until well blended.

3. Add the vanilla, pulse, and then add the dates a few at a time and pulse until the batter resembles cake crumbs. When you press it between two fingers it should stick together.

4. Press the brownie batter into the pan and refrigerate until ready to use.

5. To make the cheesecake layer: Place the cashews, coconut oil, lemon juice, maple syrup, and vanilla in a food processor and process for a few minutes, or until the mixture is creamy with no lumps.

6. Place the raspberries in a bowl and lightly crush them so they are leaking juice and in pieces. Gently stir the raspberries into the cheesecake mixture.

7. Take out the chilled brownie layer and spread the cheesecake layer over the top. Shuffle the pan in your hands to even out the cheesecake layer and place the pan in the freezer. Freeze for at least 4 hours or overnight.

8. To serve, slice the brownies straight out of the freezer, and store, covered, in the freezer.

Yield: 16 squares

Chocolate Macaroon Bars

•Gluten-Free •Grain-Free •Dairy-Free •Paleo •Nut-Free •Egg-Free

Coconut and chocolate historically make great candy bars. There are two layers to these bars: the macaroon bottom layer and the chocolate top. Together they make a simple candy bar–like treat. In warmer climates and in the summer months, I suggest storing these in the refrigerator.

The coconut milk makes these naturally dairy-free; however, if you like using heavy cream in ganache, use it in place of the coconut milk. And of course feel free to use another milk such as almond milk (page 17) or other nut or seed milk.

I prefer to use an 8-inch (20 cm) square pan, but you can use any baking pan around the same size.

FOR THE MACAROON LAYER:

1 cup (64 g) unsweetened shredded coconut

¼ cup (26 g) coconut flour

⅛ teaspoon salt

2 tablespoons (40 g) maple syrup or honey

¼ cup (57 g) unsalted butter, melted, or coconut oil or ghee

FOR THE CHOCOLATE LAYER:

1 cup (168 g) semisweet chocolate chips or other chocolate pieces

½ cup (120 ml) coconut milk

¼ teaspoon salt

1 teaspoon (5 ml) vanilla extract

1. To make the macaroon layer: Place the shredded coconut, coconut flour, and salt in a bowl and blend with a fork or spoon.

2. Add the maple syrup and butter and blend well. Let the mixture sit for a few minutes.

3. Grease an 8 × 8 × 2 inches (20 × 20 × 5 cm) baking or tart pan, and using your fingers, press the macaroon layer into the pan.

4. To make the chocolate layer: Bring some water in a saucepan to a simmer and place a glass bowl on top of it, without letting the bowl touch the water.

5. Reserve about 1 tablespoon (11 g) of the chocolate chips, then add the rest to the glass bowl and slowly melt the chocolate. When most of the chocolate is melted, turn off the heat and place the remaining chocolate in the bowl and stir to melt completely. Add the milk, salt, and vanilla, and stir to combine.

5. Cool for a moment and then pour the melted chocolate on top of the macaroon layer.

6. Chill in the refrigerator for at least 1 hour. Slice and serve. Store, covered, in the refrigerator for several weeks.

YIELD: 12 squares

CHAPTER 6

PIES AND TARTS

Here's a collection of recipes that can be used for top and bottom pie crusts, tarts, and quiches. I combine the coconut flour with blanched almond flour or almond meal in all of these recipes in varying ratios. I tend to use blanched almond flour because its color and buttery texture reminds me of traditional pastry and pie crusts that use all-purpose and pastry flours. If you prefer, you can choose another nut or seed flour, such as hazelnut, pecan, sunflower, or pumpkin seed.

Everyday Pie Crust

•Gluten-Free •Grain-Free •Low-Sugar •Dairy-Free Option •Paleo •Nut-Free Option

You can make this simple crust with almond flour or another nut or seed flour. It can also be converted into a savory crust by omitting the honey. You can add other seasonings or herbs as well, such as cinnamon for a sweet crust or minced scallions for a savory crust.

You can make this crust in an 8- or 9-inch (20 or 23 cm) round pie plate, or a similar-size tart pan.

½ cup (48 g) blanched almond flour, or other nut or seed flour

½ cup (52 g) coconut flour

¼ teaspoon salt

¼ cup (57 g) unsalted butter, or ghee, coconut oil, or palm shortening

2 eggs

1 teaspoon (7 g) honey (optional)

1. Preheat your oven to 350°F (180°C, or gas mark 4).

2. Add the almond flour, coconut flour, and salt to a bowl and blend with a fork or whisk.

3. Add the butter, eggs, and honey to the flour and stir until well blended.

4. Press the dough evenly across the bottom and sides of your pie plate.

5. Bake the crust for 10 minutes, or until it begins to brown just a bit.

6. The crust is now ready to be filled, or it can be stored in a sealed container in the refrigerator for a few days or in the freezer for a few months.

Yield: 1 single pie crust

Pastry Crust

•Gluten-Free   •Grain-Free   •Low-Sugar   •Dairy-Free Option   •Paleo

Here's a buttery soft pie crust that stays tender even after baking. I use it for quiches and other tender or light fillings and when I want a soft crust like a pastry shell. This crust fits in an 8-inch (20 cm) or 9-inch (23 cm) pie plate, or a similar-size tart pan. This crust tends to stick to the sides of pie and tart pans that are not a nonstick surface, however, so I suggest lining the pan's bottom and sides with parchment paper or greasing it generously before pressing the dough into the pan.

1¼ cup (120 g) blanched almond flour

2 tablespoons (13 g) coconut flour

½ teaspoon salt

1 large egg

¼ cup (57 g) unsalted butter, melted, or coconut oil, palm shortening, or ghee

1. Preheat your oven to 350°F (180°C, or gas mark 4).

2. Generously grease an 8-inch (20 cm) or 9-inch (23 cm) pie pan or tart pan or line it with parchment paper.

2. Add the almond flour, coconut flour, and salt to a bowl and blend with a fork or whisk. Add the egg and butter to the flour and blend well with a fork, until the dough comes together.

3. Press the dough evenly onto the bottom and sides of your pie pan.

4. Bake the crust for 10 minutes, or until it begins to brown just a bit.

5. Cool the crust and then add your pie filling. Or you can store the baked, unfilled crust in a sealed container in the refrigerator for a few days or freezer for a few weeks.

Yield: 1 single pie crust

Almond Cobbler and Pie Crust

•Gluten-Free   •Grain-Free   •Low-Sugar   •Dairy-Free Option   •Paleo   •Egg-Free

Almond flour has a buttery taste that works well as a top crust. The coconut flour works in a supporting role firming up the crust enough to give it shape and structure. If you don't have blanched almond flour, almond meal will also work with this recipe. Although this recipe is ideal for a top crust, it can sometimes be used as a bottom crust when the pie filling isn't too wet. It will likely fall apart if used as a bottom crust with a liquid filling such as the Triple Berry Cobbler (page 121); however, it can stand up to a thick quiche filling such as the Cowboy Quiche (page 123). Use the Everyday Pie Crust (page 115) if you have a liquid filling.

To make this dairy-free, use coconut oil or palm shortening in place of butter or ghee. You can also make this crust in an 8- or 9-inch (20 or 23 cm) round pie pan, or a similar-size tart pan.

1½ cups (144 g) blanched almond flour

2 tablespoons (13 g) coconut flour

¼ teaspoon salt

¼ teaspoon baking soda

¼ cup (57 g) unsalted butter, melted, or coconut oil, ghee, or palm shortening

2 tablespoons (40 g) maple syrup or honey

1 teaspoon (5 ml) vanilla extract

1. Preheat your oven to 350°F (180°C, or gas mark 4).

2. Whisk the almond flour, coconut flour, salt, and baking soda together in a bowl.

3. In a separate bowl, blend together the butter, maple syrup, and vanilla. Add it to the dry mixture and stir until well blended.

4. Press the dough evenly into a pie pan or other baking dish, as well as along the sides. Poke a few holes in the bottom of the crust with a fork, and bake for 10 minutes, or until the crust begins to turn golden.

5. Cool the crust and then add your pie filling. Or you can store the crust in a sealed container in the refrigerator for a few days or freezer for a few weeks, until you're ready to bake a pie.

Yield: 1 single pie or cobbler crust

Strawberry Rhubarb Cobbler

•Gluten-Free •Grain-Free •Low-Sugar •Dairy-Free Option •Paleo •Nut-Free •Egg-Free Option

Strawberries and rhubarb are a classic pie or cobbler mix. Rhubarb is a tart, ruby red vegetable, although some varieties are less so. The most popular varieties appear in late spring. Historically, rhubarb has been used medicinally for cleansing (it's a natural laxative), but the leaves of the plant are toxic mostly because of their high oxalate content.

2 cups chopped (244 g) rhubarb (about 1 large stalk, or two small)

1½ pounds (681 g) strawberries (about 4 cups), chopped into bite-size pieces

1 teaspoon (2 g) ground cinnamon

1 teaspoon (5 ml) lemon juice

1 teaspoon (5 ml) lemon zest (optional)

1 tablespoon (15 ml) melted ghee, butter, or coconut oil

¼ cup (80 g) honey or maple syrup

1 Almond Cobbler and Pie Crust (page 118)

2 tablespoons (28 ml) egg white (about ½ large egg white) (optional)

1. Preheat your oven to 350°F (180°C, or gas mark 4).

2. Prepare the filling by combining all the ingredients in a bowl and stirring until well blended.

3. Scoop the filling into an 8-inch (20 cm) pie dish or a similar-size tart pan.

4. Place the crust between two pieces of parchment paper and roll it out to the size that fits over the baking dish and place it on top of the filling. Tuck in any dough that is falling over the edges. Brush the egg white over the crust and punch holes in the crust with fork.

5. Bake for 35 minutes or until the crust is browned and the filling is bubbling.

6. Cool for a few minutes and serve with ice cream, whipped yogurt, or whipped cream (page 100)

Yield: 1 pie, or 8 servings

Triple Berry Cobbler

•Gluten-Free   •Grain-Free   •Dairy-Free   •Low-Sugar Option   •Paleo   •Nut-Free   •Egg-Free Option

Triple berry can become double berry or even quadruple berry depending on what's in season or what you have in your freezer. My mix usually includes blueberries, raspberries, and strawberries. You can vary the ratio of berries depending on the balance of sweetness and tartness of your berries. If using frozen berries, first thaw them completely and drain any excess liquid.

You'll notice I don't use cornstarch to thicken the berry mixture, but you can add 1 tablespoon (6 g) almond flour to thicken the filling, or boil the filling in a saucepan over medium heat for about 10 minutes, cool it a few minutes, and then pour it into your baking dish and top it with the cobbler crust. You can use a pie plate or baking dish to make this cobbler; I tend to use a 9-inch (23 cm) pie plate and treat it as a one-crust pie.

2 pounds (1 kg) berries (about 5 cups, or 2½ pints)

¼ cup (80 g) maple syrup or honey or coconut sugar (30 g), or more depending on the sweetness of the berries

¼ teaspoon salt

¼ teaspoon ground cinnamon

1 tablespoon (15 ml) lemon juice

2 tablespoons (28 ml) egg white (about ½ large egg white) (optional)

Almond Cobbler and Pie Crust (page 118)

1. Preheat your oven to 350°F (180°C, or gas mark 4).

2. Combine the berries, maple syrup, salt, cinnamon, and lemon juice in a bowl and blend gently with a spoon or spatula.

3. Scoop the berry filling into a pie plate or baking dish.

4. Place the cobbler crust between two pieces of parchment paper and roll it out to the size that fits over the baking dish and place it on top of the filling. Pinch the corners with your fingers to seal the crust around the edges. Brush the egg white over the crust and poke holes in the crust with a fork.

5. Place the cobbler into the oven and place a baking sheet under it to catch any drips. Bake for 30 minutes, or until the filling is bubbling and the crust is browned.

6. Cool for a few minutes and serve. Store at room temperature for a few days or in the refrigerator for a week or so.

Yield: 1 pie, or 8 servings

LOW-SUGAR AND EGG-FREE OPTIONS

To make this low-sugar, replace the ¼ cup (80 g) of the maple syrup with ½ teaspoon stevia powder. To make this egg-free, omit the egg wash.

Cowboy Quiche

•Gluten-Free   •Grain-Free   •Low-Sugar   •Nut-Free

I'm a city kid by birth, but since moving to the West Coast. I've grown to appreciate the cowboy and cowgirl culture. I was inspired by a couple of recipes I've seen by the same name to create this recipe. I suspect cowboys and cowgirls of all ages will love this one, especially anyone who loves a hardy breakfast in a single slice of goodness. For the sausage, you can use bulk chicken, pork, or turkey sausage, or take sausage out of its casings. Another option is to use 8 slices of bacon, chopped into pieces, in place of the sausage. Use your favorite cheese, stay with cheddar, or mix it up with some Monterey Jack cheese.

2 tablespoons (28 g) ghee, unsalted butter, coconut oil, or other oil

1 large yellow onion, sliced into thin strips

½ pound (227 g) bulk seasoned sausage

6 large eggs

⅓ cup (77 g) yogurt, sour cream, or heavy cream

1½ cups (170 g) shredded sharp cheddar cheese or other cheese

¼ teaspoon salt

Dash Tabasco sauce or pinch cayenne pepper

Salt and pepper

Everyday Pie Crust (page 115), Pastry Crust (page 117), or Almond Cobbler and Pie Crust (page 118)

1. Preheat a skillet on a medium heat and add the ghee and onions. Cook the onions, stirring occasionally, for 10 minutes, or until they begin to caramelize. Place the onions in a large mixing bowl.

2. Add the sausage to the skillet and cook over medium heat for 5 minutes, or until they're browned and almost completely cooked.

3. Add the sausage to the onions, and stir in the eggs, yogurt, cheese, salt, and Tabasco sauce. Season with salt and pepper.

4. Press the pie crust into an 8-inch (20 cm) or 9-inch (23 cm) pie or tart pan. Add the sausage mixture and bake for 30 minutes, or until the center of the quiche is cooked and not transparent.

5. Cool for a minute and serve. Store, covered, in the refrigerator for a few days or in the freezer for a few months.

Yield: 1 quiche, or 6 servings

Spinach Feta Quiche

•Gluten-Free   •Grain-Free   •Low-Sugar

I love green food. I was the kid who liked broccoli, spinach, squash, and Brussels sprouts. My perfect quick meal is sautéed spinach with onions, olive oil, cheese, and 2 eggs—basically the filling for spanakopita, or Greek spinach pie. The only difference in this version is I add roasted cherry tomatoes for an additional pop of flavor. When I can't find local feta cheese, I buy cheese made from sheep's milk (Valbreso Feta) imported from France, but any brand will work, and you may be lucky enough to find some locally produced feta cheese. I've been able to find local feta from time to time at my local market. Finally, if you're using frozen spinach, drain any excess water before chopping and adding it.

Pastry Crust (page 117) or Almond Cobbler and Pie Crust (page 118)

2 tablespoons (28 g) olive oil, ghee, or other oil

1 medium onion, peeled and finely diced

10 ounces (283 g) chopped fresh or frozen spinach

7 ounces (198 g) feta cheese

2 eggs, whisked

1 tablespoon (4 g) fresh herbs such as dill or oregano (optional)

1 cup (420 g) Roasted Cherry Tomatoes (page 152)

1. Preheat your oven to 350°F (180°C, or gas mark 4).

2. Press the pie crust into an 8-inch (20 cm) or 9-inch (23 cm) pie pan or similar-size tart pan or baking dish. Bake for 10 minutes and then cool while you prepare the filling.

3. Preheat a skillet over medium heat and add the olive oil, onions, and spinach. Sauté, stirring occasionally, for 5 to 8 minutes, or until the onions are turning translucent.

4. Turn off the heat and add the feta cheese and eggs; stir to blend well. Add the herbs and mix well. Finally stir in the roasted tomatoes.

5. Pour the spinach mixture into the pie crust and bake for 20 minutes, or until the filling is fully baked.

6. Serve warm or at room temperature. Store, covered, in the refrigerator for a few days or in the freezer for a few months.

Yield: 1 quiche

CHAPTER 7

SOUPS AND SMOOTHIES

Soups and smoothies are great sources of vegetable and fruit fibers, vitamins, minerals, and immune-boosting ingredients. Blending or cooking a small amount of coconut flour into a smoothie or soup boosts the fiber and protein source, thickens it, and removes any grainy texture from the coconut fibers in the flour. I use a high-speed Vitamix blender to obtain a super smooth consistency, but any high-speed blender or food processor will work.

Soups and stews are another great source of nourishment for meals and snacks. Cooked or cold puréed soups with a small amount of coconut flour added boosts the level of protein and natural fiber and helps to thicken otherwise thin stocks and soups. To get these benefits cook it for at least 5 minutes, otherwise make sure to blend or purée the flour into the soup to remove any fiber texture.

Chocolate Recovery Shake

•Gluten-Free   •Grain-Free   •Dairy-Free   •Low-Sugar   •Paleo   •Nut-Free Option   •Egg-Free

Within an hour of a hard workout I try to replenish my body with recovery food, usually a banana, fruit bar, or smoothie, and this chocolate shake is like having your cake and eating it, too. It's creamy but not too heavy and is a balanced source of vitamins, minerals, protein, good fat, and carbohydrates.

If you use a frozen banana in this shake, it will require less ice and the shake will be slightly thicker and creamier. The small amount of coconut flour adds fiber, and the almond butter adds protein as well.

1 cup (235 ml) coconut milk or other dairy-free milk

1 ripe banana (about 100g), peeled

1½ ounces (40 g) Medjool dates, pitted (about 2 dates), or 1 tablespoon (20 g) honey or maple syrup

2 tablespoons (11 g) unsweetened cocoa or cacao

2 tablespoons (32 g) almond butter or other nut or seed butter

½ teaspoon coconut flour

1 cup (120 g) of ice

Place all the ingredients in a blender and blend until smooth.

Yield: About 1½ cups (350 ml), or 1 serving

Orange Immune-Boosting Smoothie

•Gluten-Free •Grain-Free •Dairy-Free •Low-Sugar •Paleo •Nut-Free •Egg-Free

A naturally sweet citrus smoothie can easily turn into an immune-boosting smoothie, packed with essential vitamins and minerals, including A, B-6, C, and magnesium, thanks to the oranges and pineapple. If you're using frozen pineapple you may be able to use less ice depending on how much juice you get from your oranges. Add one of the immune-boosting ingredients to the base of this recipe for an even more charged smoothie.

2 medium oranges, peeled and roughly chopped

1 cup (165 g) fresh or frozen chopped pineapple pieces

½ teaspoon coconut flour

1 cup (120 g) ice

1 teaspoon immune booster (see sidebar at right)

Place all the ingredients in the container of a high-speed blender and blend until smooth.

Yield: About 1½ cups (350 ml), or 1 serving

SMOOTHIE IMMUNE BOOSTERS

There are a variety of immune-boosting ingredients you can add to your smoothie. What one you choose will depend in part on the flavor it imparts, the other ingredients in your smoothie, and what benefits you're looking to boost. Here's a summary of some options and what they deliver.

Manuka honey: This is honey that's highly bioactive with good bacteria making it antibacterial and antiviral.

Ginger (freshly grated): This is a natural anti-inflammatory agent and digestive movement and motility agent.

Turmeric (freshly grated): This is a natural anti-inflammatory and antiviral agent.

Greens powder: These dried greens are superfood mixtures that provide many of the benefits you receive when eating green vegetables. See Resources (page 154) for my preferred brand.

Banana Porridge

•Gluten-Free •Grain-Free •Dairy-Free •Low-Sugar •Paleo •Nut-Free •Egg-Free Option

Porridge usually uses grains such as wheat or oatmeal, which give it a nice thick texture. This grain-free porridge has a true porridge texture and flavor, with a subtle sweetness thanks to the banana and cinnamon. To make this egg-free, just omit the eggs and cook a bit longer, or add an egg-replacer such as flaxseed meal (see page 18 for substitution specifics). This is naturally dairy-free but you can also use dairy-based milk if you prefer.

½ cup (120 ml) coconut milk or other milk

½ cup (120 ml) water

¼ cup (26 g) coconut flour

1 very ripe banana, mashed

½ teaspoon ground cinnamon

¼ teaspoon salt

2 large eggs, lightly beaten

1. Place the coconut milk and water in a saucepan over medium-low heat.

2. Add the coconut flour to the saucepan and stir to blend.

3. Add the mashed banana to the saucepan and stir to blend.

4. Add the cinnamon and salt to the saucepan and blend well.

5. Add the eggs to the saucepan and blend. Stir occasionally for a few minutes, or until the porridge becomes thick and a bit lumpy.

6. Serve warm or at room temperature. Leftovers may be stored in a sealed container in the refrigerator for a few days and reheated before serving.

Yield: About 2 cups (446 g), or 2 servings

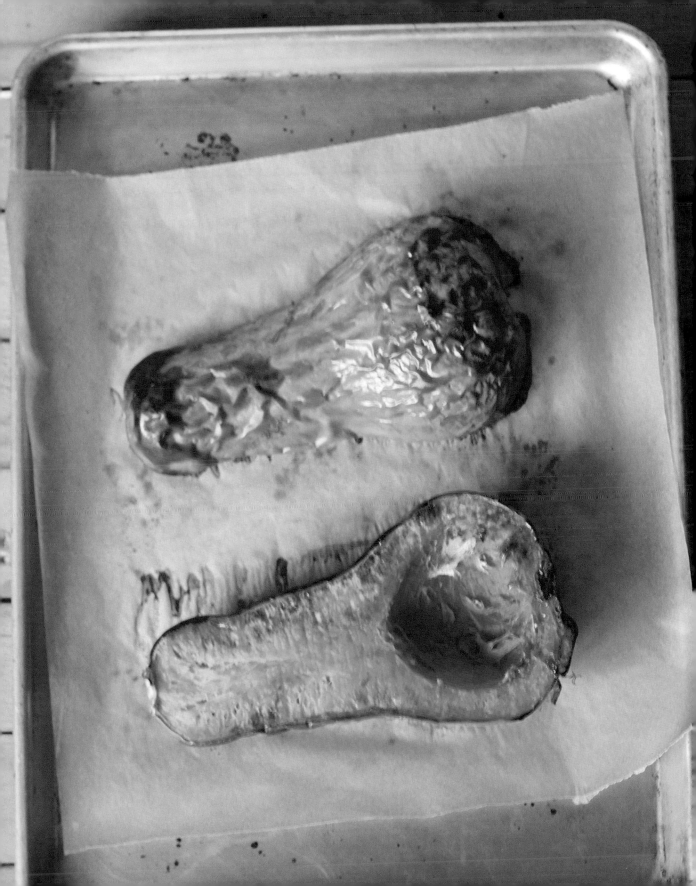

Roasted Butternut Squash Soup

▾Gluten-Free ▾Grain-Free ▾Low-Sugar ▾Paleo ▾Nut-Free ▾Egg-Free

Butternut squash offers a solid punch of the vitamins found in orange-colored foods. It's loaded with vitamin A and C, with some iron and calcium thrown in for good measure. Unlike citrus fruits with a similar vitamin profile, it's not acidic, which makes it quite gentle on sensitive digestive systems. And another amazing fact? Butternut squash seems to last for months without going bad—I've used one up to 3 months old. I'm not sure how much longer it can keep, but I store mine in a dry, cool, dark place.

2 tablespoons (28 g) unsalted butter, ghee, or coconut oil

1 medium yellow onion, peeled and diced

2½ cups (570 ml) chicken broth (page 134), vegetable broth, or water

4 large garlic cloves, peeled and minced

3 cups (720 g) roasted, diced butternut squash (see below), warmed

1. Preheat a skillet on a medium heat and add the butter. Add the onions to the skillet and cook, stirring occasionally, until they begin to brown and caramelize.

2. In the meantime, bring the broth to a simmer in a saucepan over low heat. Then place the garlic in the pan and cook another few minutes, or until the garlic become fragrant.

3. Place the butternut squash, onions, garlic, and chicken broth in a blender and blend until smooth.

4. Serve warm. Store in a sealed container in the refrigerator for a few days or in the freezer for a few months.

Yield: 4 servings

HOW TO ROAST BUTTERNUT SQUASH

Here's a simple method for making roasted squash that can be used in this recipe as well as the Spiced Pumpkin Bread on page 48.

Preheat your oven to 400°F (200°C, or gas mark 6). Slice one butternut squash in half lengthwise, and then scoop out the seeds. Rub the inside of each squash half with coconut oil, ghee, or other high-heat oil, and place on a greased or parchment-lined baking sheet, cut side up. Roast for about 30 minutes, or until the squash is tender and you can insert a fork in the thickest part.

Cool, and then cut into cubes for recipes needing diced cooked squash. To make purée, scoop out the squash and purée it in a blender. If it's dry you may need to add a bit of water. Leftover squash may be kept in a sealed container in the refrigerator for a few days or in the freezer for a few months.

Dumpling (Matzo Ball) Soup

•Gluten-Free •Grain-Free •Low-Sugar •Dairy-Free Option •Paleo •Nut-Free

Matzo ball soup (Jewish chicken soup with dumplings) is a blend of comfort food and nour-ishment. If you don't eat chicken, you can use these dumplings in any soup or stew, or add them to a vegetable broth. The technique for making these dumplings using coconut flour is to bake instead of boil them, which ensures that the dough doesn't fall apart in the soup and also means you can make the soup separately.

To make these dairy-free, use chicken fat, duck fat, coconut oil, or palm shortening. If you don't have fresh herbs on hand, use a teaspoon of dried herbs such as thyme and rosemary.

4 eggs

¼ cup (57 g) unsalted butter, melted, or chicken fat, duck fat, ghee or coconut oil

¼ teaspoon salt

¼ teaspoon baking soda

⅓ cup (35 g) coconut flour

1 tablespoon (2.5 g) mixed minced fresh herbs such as rosemary, sage, and thyme

8 cups (2 L) chicken broth (page 134)

1. Preheat your oven to 350°F (180°C, or gas mark 4).

2. Line a baking sheet with parchment paper or a nonstick surface.

3. Whisk the eggs and butter together in a bowl. Add the salt, baking soda, coconut flour, and herbs to the egg mixture and whisk until blended. Let the batter sit for a few minutes to thicken and blend once more.

4. Drop 1 to 2 tablespoons (15 to 28 ml) of batter about an inch (2.5 cm) apart onto the baking sheet and bake for 10 minutes, or until the edges start to turn gold.

5. Heat the chicken broth.

6. To serve, pour about 2 cups (475 ml) hot chicken broth into a soup bowl and add 2 to 3 dumplings.

7. Store the dumplings separately from the soup to keep them from getting soggy. Store in a sealed container at room temperature for a few days, in the refrigerator for a few weeks, or in the freezer for a few months. To rewarm the dumplings, place them in simmering soup or stew for a few minutes and serve.

Yield: About 10 dumplings, or 4 servings

Bonus Recipe: Chicken Broth

•Gluten-Free   •Grain Free   •Low-Sugar   •Dairy-Free   •Paleo   •Nut-Free

Chicken broth is so soothing to the body and soul. Have it on its own as a soup or use it to build nutritious soups, stews, puréed vegetables, and other recipes that call for savory liquids (like the two preceding this recipe).

I freeze chicken broth in 2-cup (475 ml) portions because this size is easy to add to recipes or to make a big bowl of soup. You may find it helpful to freeze smaller amounts of broth in an ice cube tray for adding a bit of flavor to a marinade, soup, or sauce. Label your containers and keep them in the freezer for up to a few months. When freezing the broth in a jar or other container, leave some space at the top to allow for expansion as the liquid freezes.

Leftover chicken bones, chicken pieces, or a chicken carcass

8 cups (2 L) water or enough to cover most of the chicken

4 cups (520 g) diced vegetables or vegetable scraps (e.g., carrots, celery, leeks, onions; avoid cabbage, which tends to make the broth bitter)

Chopped herbs or other seasonings (e.g., thyme, parsley, chives, garlic, green onions)

Kosher or sea salt and pepper (optional)

1 tablespoon (15 ml) apple cider vinegar (optional)

1. Place the chicken in a stockpot or slow cooker and fill with the water, enough to cover most of the chicken.

2. Add diced vegetables and herbs and other seasonings; season to taste with salt and pepper. Add the vinegar to help extract minerals, such as calcium, from the chicken bones.

3. Simmer, covered, over low heat for at least 3 hours in a stockpot, up to 1 hour in a pressure cooker, or up to 10 hours in a slow cooker.

4. Turn off the heat and let the chicken soup cool until you can handle it, and then strain the liquid through a fine-mesh strainer. Discard everything but the broth.

5. Store the broth in a sealed container in the refrigerator for up to a week, or in the freezer for several months.

Yield: About 8 cups (2 L)

CHAPTER 8

SAVORY BITES AND MEALS

These savory recipes offer a range of options and ideas for incorporating coconut flour into your meals. Coconut flour can be used to seal in the juices before searing, and for sautéing, roasting, or baking poultry, seafood, and other ingredients. It's great for making thin, light crêpes and tortillas as well as in heartier fare such as the Salmon Croquettes with Lemon–Dill Yogurt Sauce (page 150), Scallion Pancakes with Soy Ginger Sauce (page 141), and Fennel Pesto Meatballs (page 151). I like to use coconut flour in combination with almond flour to get the best flavor and texture in breaded or floured food, as in the Chicken Strips (page 153). You can also thicken the texture of a dish by adding a bit of coconut flour, as I do in the Shepherd's Pie (page 147) and Sloppy Joes (page 145). The options are endless!

Chicken Piccata

•Gluten-Free •Grain-Free •Low-Sugar •Dairy-Free Option •Paleo •Egg-Free

Lemon, olive oil, butter, and capers make a savory sauce for this pan-fried "breaded" chicken cutlet entrée. Serve this over rice, quinoa, or noodles and pour the lemon sauce over the entire dish to spread the flavor throughout.

The technique for butterflying a chicken breast is not as hard as it sounds. Lay the boneless chicken breast flat on a cutting board. Placing one hand on the chicken and holding a knife in the other, with the blade parallel to the cutting board, cut across the inside of the breast most of the way, leaving the last part intact. Open up the chicken and cut to separate it into two pieces. Do the same for the other chicken breast to get four chicken cutlets.

To make this dairy-free you can substitute more olive oil or sunflower oil for the butter.

2 large boneless, skinless chicken breasts (about 1½ pounds, or 680 g), butterflied and cut in half to make 4 chicken cutlets

Salt and pepper

¼ cup (24 g) blanched almond flour or other nut or seed flour

2 tablespoons (13 g) coconut flour

¼ cup (57 g) unsalted butter or ghee, divided

¼ cup (60 ml) olive oil, divided

⅓ cup (80 ml) fresh lemon juice

½ cup (120 ml) chicken stock

¼ cup (34 g) brined capers, drained and rinsed

¼ cup (15 g) chopped fresh parsley

1. Season the chicken cutlets lightly with salt and pepper.

2. Mix the almond flour and coconut flour together in a bowl until well blended. Place the flour mixture on a plate. Dredge the chicken pieces in the flour and shake off the excess flour and set aside.

3. Warm a large skillet over medium-high heat and melt 2 tablespoons (28 g) of the butter plus 2 tablespoons (28 ml) of the olive oil until bubbling.

4. Place two pieces of chicken in the skillet and brown for a few minutes on each side. Transfer to a warm plate.

5. Add the remaining 2 tablespoons (28 g) butter and 2 tablespoons (28 ml) olive oil. Melt and heat to bubbling, and brown the other 2 chicken pieces. Move them to the plate as well.

6. Add the lemon juice, stock, and capers to the skillet and bring to a boil. Deglaze by scraping the brown bits from the pan.

7. Place all the chicken cutlets in the skillet and simmer for 5 to 7 minutes, or until the chicken is tender and cooked through.

8. Garnish with parsley and serve with rice, quinoa, or roasted riced cauliflower.

Yield: 4 servings

Coconut Shrimp with Sweet Chili Dipping Sauce

•Gluten-Free   •Grain-Free   •Dairy-Free   •Paleo   •Nut-Free   •Egg-Free Option

This recipe was inspired by a recipe I found on the Skinny Taste website www.skinnytaste .com. I make this recipe when I have access to fresh or frozen wild and sustainable shrimp. I set up an assembly line of bowls for dipping each shrimp in the flour, egg, and coconut, and then slide them into the oven to bake up a crunchy coconut shell around the shrimp.

Here's the dipping sequence for the shrimp: coconut flour + salt → egg → shredded coconut → bake.

I keep the seasoning here pretty basic, but in addition to the salt, you could add chili powder or onion and garlic powder to the coconut flour. I use unsweetened shredded coconut here, but feel free to use sweetened if you prefer. See Resources, (page 154) for my preferred brand of shredded coconut. If you don't have apricot preserves, orange marmalade, peach preserves, other stone fruit, or citrus preserves will work.

To make this egg-free, eliminate the egg and blend the shredded coconut, salt, and coconut flour in a bowl, dredge each shrimp in the mixture, and bake.

FOR THE DIPPING SAUCE:

½ cup (160 g) apricot preserves or other stone fruit or citrus preserves

1 tablespoon (15 ml) rice vinegar or other vinegar

¼ teaspoon crushed red pepper flakes (optional)

FOR THE SHRIMP:

¼ teaspoon salt

¼ cup (26 g) coconut flour

1 large egg

½ cup (32 g) unsweetened shredded coconut

1 pound (454 g) large raw shrimp (about 20 shrimp), peeled and deveined

1. Preheat your oven to 425°F (220°C, or gas mark 7).

2. Line a baking sheet with parchment paper or other nonstick surface.

3. To make the dipping sauce: Add all the ingredients in a small bowl and blend with a fork or spoon. Set aside.

4. To make the shrimp: In one small bowl whisk together the salt and the coconut flour. In a separate bowl whisk the egg. Place the shredded coconut in a third bowl.

5. Dip each shrimp in the coconut flour; shake off excess flour, and then dip in the egg to coat it. Let excess egg drip off, and then dip the shrimp in the shredded coconut on both sides to coat. Place the coated shrimp on the baking sheet and repeat for the remaining shrimp.

6. Bake the shrimp on one side for 10 minutes, and then turn each shrimp over and bake for another 10 minutes, or until the edges of the coconut are browned.

7. Serve warm or at room temperature with the dipping sauce. Store, covered, in the refrigerator for a few days and reheat at 400°F (200°C, or gas mark 6) for 6 minutes.

Yield: 20 large shrimp, or 4 servings

Scallion Pancakes with Soy Ginger Sauce

•Gluten-Free •Grain-Free •Dairy-Free •Paleo •Nut-Free

Scallions are a great addition to savory dishes, especially savory pancakes. In this recipe the coconut flour is a supporting player, helping to thicken the patties to balance out the moist addition of sesame oil and either soy sauce or coconut aminos.

This recipe can be served as an appetizer or as a meal on top of an Asian-style salad or with rice, or it can be eaten as an Asian patty on a bun. Don't pass up the soy ginger sauce thinking that it will take too long to make. It's worth the extra effort and can simmer while you're making the pancakes.

FOR THE SOY GINGER SAUCE:

¼ cup (80 g) maple syrup, honey, or coconut sugar (30 g)

¼ cup (60 ml) water

¼ cup (60 ml) gluten-free soy sauce, coconut aminos, or ½ teaspoon salt

2 tablespoons (12 g) chopped fresh ginger

½ teaspoon ground coriander

FOR THE PANCAKES:

5 scallions

1 cup (16 g) cilantro or other herb, such as arugula or parsley

1 pound (454 g) ground chicken breast, pork, or turkey

1 large egg

2 tablespoons (28 ml) toasted sesame oil

2 tablespoons (28 ml) gluten-free soy sauce or coconut aminos or ½ teaspoon salt

1 tablespoon (7 g) coconut flour

2 tablespoons (28 ml) cooking oil

1. To make the soy ginger sauce: Add the maple syrup, water, soy sauce, ginger, and coriander to a saucepan and simmer for 30 minutes, or until the liquid is reduced by about half.

2. Cool the sauce and pour it through a fine-mesh strainer to remove the ginger and coriander. The sauce will be slightly thickened and syrupy when cooled.

3. To make the pancakes: Finely mince the scallions and cilantro, using a knife or a food processor.

4. Add the scallions, cilantro, and chicken to a bowl and mix well.

5. Add the egg, sesame oil, soy sauce, and coconut flour to the chicken mixture and blend well.

6. Preheat a large skillet over medium heat and add the cooking oil. Using an ice cream scoop or large spoon, scoop out between 1 to 2 tablespoons (between 14 and 28 g) of the chicken mixture and drop into skillet. Flatten a bit with the spoon to create a small pancake. Cook each pancake about 5 minutes on each side, or until they are browning.

7. Place cooked pancakes on a paper towel over a warm plate and continue with the remaining batter.

8. Serve warm with soy ginger sauce. Store in a sealed container in the refrigerator for a few days or in the freezer for a few weeks. The sauce can be stored, covered, in the refrigerator for several weeks.

Yield: About 16 pancakes, or 3 to 4 servings

Chili-Lime Chicken Quesadillas

•Gluten-Free •Grain-Free •Low-Sugar •Nut-Free

My favorite spice to make from scratch is ancho chili powder—a black, relatively mild chili spice with a deep color and flavor. To make it, toast a dried ancho chili pepper, and then grind it into a powder using a spice or coffee grinder. If you can't find it, just use additional red chili powder.

FOR THE CHICKEN:

3 tablespoons (45 ml) cooking oil, divided

1½ pounds (680 g) boneless, skinless chicken breasts

½ teaspoon salt

1 teaspoon (2.6 g) chili powder

1 teaspoon (2.6 g) ancho chili powder (or substitute more chili powder)

1 teaspoon (2.5 g) coconut sugar or other sweetener

1 tablespoon (15 ml) lime juice

FOR THE QUESADILLAS:

12 tortillas (page 37; double the recipe)

2 cups (200 g) Monterey Jack, pepper Jack, or other cheese

1. Warm a grill or skillet over medium heat. If using a skillet, add 1 tablespoon (15 ml) of the cooking oil to it.

2. To make the chicken: Add the chicken, salt, chili powders, coconut sugar, the remaining 2 tablespoons (28 ml) cooking oil, and lime juice to a bowl and marinate for at least 10 minutes, or up to 12 hours in the refrigerator.

3. In the skillet or on the grill, cook the chili chicken about 5 minutes on each side, or until cooked through.

4. Cool and cut the chicken up into bite-size pieces.

5. To assemble the quesadillas: Warm a skillet over medium heat and place 1 tortilla in the skillet. Top with some chicken and cheese. Place another tortilla over it and press down with a spatula. Cook the quesadilla about 5 minutes, or until the cheese has melted and the top and bottom tortilla stay together. Flip the tortilla over and cook for another few minutes. Repeat for the remaining tortillas.

6. Slice the quesadillas into halves or quarters and serve warm with Pico de Gallo (see below).

Yield: 6 servings

PICO DE GALLO

2 large tomatoes (the sweeter the better), roughly chopped

½ cup (80 g) roughly chopped red onion

1 garlic clove

¼ cup (4 g) fresh cilantro

1 tablespoon (15 ml) fresh lime juice

1. Dice the tomatoes, onion, garlic, and cilantro with a knife, or add them to a food processor and pulse until the ingredients are chopped into salsa. Add the lime juice and blend well.

2. Serve chilled or at room temperature. Store, covered, in the refrigerator for a few days.

Yield: 2 cups (520 g)

Roasted Tomato and Pepper Jack Quesadillas

•Gluten-Free •Grain-Free •Low-Sugar •Nut-Free •Egg-Free

Here's a vegetarian quesadilla recipe that can be made using Roasted Cherry Tomatoes (page 152), Pico de Gallo (page 143), or other roasted vegetables or leftovers you have hanging around. You can put many of your favorite foods or leftovers in a quesadilla, whether they're vegetarian or not. Quesadillas are quite versatile for a variety of meals and lifestyles. I hope you'll feel inspired to invent your own quesadilla!

1 tablespoon (15 ml) ghee or coconut oil, or more as needed

6 tortillas (page 37)

1 cup (150 g) Roasted Cherry Tomatoes (page 152)

2 cups (200 g) shredded or grated Monterey Jack cheese or pepper Jack cheese

1. Preheat a skillet on a medium heat and add the 1 tablespoon (15 ml) ghee or coconut oil, enough to moisten the surface of the skillet.

2. Place a tortilla in the skillet and then add the tomatoes and cheese on top of the tortilla. Place another tortilla on top of the tomatoes and cheese and press down with a spatula to cook the quesadilla until the cheese has begun to melt and the top and bottom tortilla stay together.

3. Flip the quesadilla and cook on the other side for a minute or so, pressing down with the spatula to seal it closed with the melted cheese. Repeat for the remaining tortillas.

4. Serve warm. Store leftovers, covered, in the refrigerator for a few days.

Yield: 3 quesadillas

Sloppy Joes

•Gluten-Free   •Grain-Free   •Dairy-Free   •Low-Sugar   •Paleo   •Nut-Free   •Egg-Free

Sloppy Joes are traditionally a thick beef mixture served on a sandwich roll, but this version can be served in a bowl with a Drop Biscuit (page 41) or Garlic Cheddar Biscuit (page 43), on top of whipped or baked potatoes, alongside steamed vegetables, or as a hardy stew, with a salad on the side. To make this low-sugar, in place of the ketchup use ½ cup (120 ml) tomato sauce, 2 tablespoons (40 g) honey, and ½ teaspoon apple cider vinegar.

2 tablespoons (28 ml) coconut oil or other cooking oil

2 celery stalks, trimmed and finely diced

1 cup (200 g) finely diced onion

½ cup (100 g) finely diced carrots

2 garlic cloves, peeled and minced

1 pound (454 g) ground beef, chicken, or turkey

½ cup ketchup

½ cup (120 ml) tomato sauce

1 tablespoon (15 ml) gluten-free Worcestershire, barbecue, or steak sauce (optional)

¼ cup (60 ml) water

¼ teaspoon salt

Pinch cayenne pepper (less than ⅛ teaspoon; optional)

1 to 2 teaspoons (2 to 5 g) coconut flour

1. Heat a large skillet or sauté pan on a medium heat and add the oil.

2. Add the celery, onions, and carrots to the skillet and cook, tossing occasionally, for about 7 minutes, or until the carrots are beginning to soften and the onions are becoming translucent.

3. Add the garlic into the pan and toss with the vegetables. Cook for 1 minute.

4. Push the vegetables off to the side and place the meat in the middle of the pan. Use a spatula to break up the meat and let it sear on one side for about 4 minutes.

5. Break up the meat some more, and toss the vegetables and meat together in the pan.

6. Add the ketchup, tomato sauce, Worchestershire sauce, water, salt, and 1 teaspoon (2 g) of the coconut flour and stir to blend. Turn the heat down to medium-low.

7. Let the mixture simmer for 10 minutes or until the carrots and celery are soft. If the consistency is too wet for you, add 1 teaspoon (2 g) coconut flour and simmer 3 minutes more. If it's too dry, add a bit more water.

8. Serve warm. Store in a sealed container in the refrigerator for a few days or in the freezer for a few months.

Yield: 4 servings

Shepherd's Pie

•Gluten-Free   •Grain-Free   •Dairy-Free Option   •Low-Sugar   •Paleo   •Nut-Free   •Egg-Free

This shepherd's pie is low-carb thanks to the mashed cauliflower instead of the usual mashed potatoes, but you can certainly use mashed potatoes or other mashed root instead of the cauliflower if you prefer. The filling for the pie is actually my Sloppy Joes recipe (page 145), but other fillings will work, too, such as leftover condensed soups, stews, and diced roasted meat and gravy. Or if you're a vegetarian, lentil soup or stew works well with the cauliflower topping. I usually use an 8-inch (20 cm) round pie dish for this recipe, but a square one works as well.

2¼ pounds (1 kg) cauliflower (1 medium head), trimmed and cut into chunks

2 tablespoons (28 g) unsalted butter, ghee, or coconut oil

½ teaspoon salt, plus more to taste

1 to 2 tablespoons (15 to 28 ml) coconut milk or other kind of milk or water, or as needed to cream the cauliflower

One batch Sloppy Joes filling (page 145)

1. Steam or boil the cauliflower until it is tender and a fork easily glides into it.

2. Preheat your oven to 400°F (200°C, or gas mark 6).

3. Cool the cauliflower for a few minutes and then place it in a food processor or high-speed blender. Add the butter, salt, and 1 tablespoon (15 ml) of the milk, and blend until it is creamy. Add more milk in small increments only as needed to fully cream the cauliflower. Season to taste with salt and pepper.

4. Place the Sloppy Joes mixture in a baking pan or pie dish and spread the creamed cauliflower evenly across the top. Sprinkle the top with salt and pepper and bake for 15 minutes, or until the pie is bubbling.

5. Serve warm. Store, covered, in the refrigerator for a few days.

Yield: One 8-inch (20 cm) pie, or 4 servings

Mexican Lasagna

•Gluten-Free •Grain-Free •Low-Sugar •Nut-Free

Traditionally, lasagna is made with wide pasta noodles; however, coconut flour crêpes or tortillas are used here in their place. The Tortillas recipe (page 37) is already seasoned well for this dish, but if you prefer to use the Savory Crêpe recipe (page 73), just season it with ⅛ teaspoon salt and ¼ teaspoon cumin and a squeeze of lime juice (about 1 teaspoon, or 5 ml).

5 ounces (142 g) spinach leaves

1 cup (40 g) loosely packed cilantro

4 scallions, trimmed

1 tablespoon (15 ml) coconut oil or other cooking oil

½ pound (225 g) ground chicken, turkey, or beef

⅛ teaspoon salt, for the chicken

¼ teaspoon chili powder

¼ teaspoon cumin

¼ teaspoon salt

1 can (14.5 ounce, or 411 g) fire-roasted diced tomatoes with green chilies, or add green chilies separately (see Resources, page 154)

2 cups (200 g) shredded or grated Monterey Jack cheese or pepper Jack cheese

⅛ teaspoon hot sauce or cayenne pepper (optional)

6 to 8 tortillas (page 37) or Savory Crêpes (page 73)

1. Preheat your oven to 425°F (220°C, or gas mark 7).

2. Finely chop the spinach, cilantro, and scallions, or place the cilantro and scallions in a food processor and pulse. Add the spinach, pulsing until chopped. Set aside.

3. Place a large saucepan over a medium heat. Add the oil and the ground chicken. Break up the chicken with a spatula as it cooks. Cook the chicken for a few minutes, or until it's almost done. Remove it from the saucepan and set aside on a warm plate.

4. Add the chopped spinach, cilantro, and scallions to the saucepan, then add the chili powder, cumin, salt, and fire-roasted tomatoes. If you're adding the chilies separately, add them now as well. Cook over a medium heat for 5 minutes, stirring occasionally, and then turn off the heat.

5. In all the lasagna will have three layers. To make the first layer, place about two tortillas in an 8 × 8 × 2-inch (20 × 20 × 5 cm) baking dish, so they cover the bottom of the dish (you can cut to fit). Spoon one-third of the chicken mixture on top of the tortillas and then sprinkle on one-third of the cheese. Cover with a second layer of tortillas and repeat with another one-third chicken mixture and one-third cheese. Add the last two tortillas, then the remaining chicken mixture and the rest of the cheese.

6. Bake for 10 minutes, or until it is bubbling and the cheese is browning.

7. Cool for a few minutes and slice. Serve warm. Store, covered, in the refrigerator for a few days or in the freezer for a few months.

Yield: 6 to 8 servings

Salmon Croquettes with Lemon-Dill Yogurt Sauce

•Gluten-Free •Grain-Free •Low-Sugar •Paleo •Nut-Free

Salmon is a superfood rich in essential oils and healthy protein. I suggest using wild-caught salmon, whether fresh or canned, for the best quality and flavor. The croquettes go well with a variety of meals, on salads, and in sandwiches. This recipe makes a meal for two people or appetizers for four, so you can easily double it if you're serving it as a main course.

1½ cups (453 g) cooked salmon fillet or canned salmon

½ cup (115 g) plain yogurt

¼ cup (25 g) diced scallions

2 tablespoons (28 m l) lime juice

2 teaspoons (8 g) Dijon mustard

1 large egg

1 tablespoon (7 g) coconut flour

2 tablespoons (28 ml) coconut oil, ghee, or other cooking oil

1. In a bowl, mix together the salmon, yogurt, scallions, lime juice, mustard, and egg until well blended.

2. Add the coconut flour and blend well again. Let the salmon mixture sit for a few minutes and blend once more.

3. Heat a large skillet or sauté pan on a medium heat and add 1 tablespoon (15 ml) of the oil.

4. Using an ice cream scoop or large spoon, spoon out 2 tablespoons (28 ml) of the batter and drop it into the pan. Press it down a bit with the spoon to form the shape of a patty about 2 inches (5 cm) in diameter. Repeat for the remaining croquettes. Add another tablespoons of coconut oil if needed.

5. Cook the croquettes until brown and firm enough to flip, about 5 minutes on each side.

6. Serve warm. Store in a sealed container in the refrigerator for a few days.

Yield: 6 to 8 croquettes

LEMON-DILL YOGURT SAUCE

This sauce is a great complement to the salmon croquettes as well as to other fish dishes. Keep it chilled until you're ready to serve it. To make this dairy-free use a dairy-free yogurt.

½ cup (115 g) plain yogurt

1 garlic clove, peeled and minced

2 teaspoon (6 g) capers, drained and rinsed

2 teaspoons (10 ml) lemon juice

1 tablespoon (4 g) chopped fresh dill

1. Place all the ingredients in a bowl and stir to blend well.

2. Chill until ready to serve. Store in a sealed container in the refrigerator for a few days.

Yield: ½ cup (125 g)

Fennel Pesto Meatballs

•Gluten-Free •Grain-Free •Low-Sugar •Dairy-Free Option •Paleo •Nut-Free

These healthy meatballs pack great flavor thanks to the fennel seeds and pesto, and have some added fiber to boot thanks to the coconut flour. This is also a great meal to prepare ahead of time, and reheat at a moment's notice. Add your favorite sauce (the Tomato Chutney on page 152 is a great choice) then place on top of spaghetti squash or gluten-free pasta for a complete meal.

½ cup (113 g) prepared pesto (page 35)

1 tablespoon (6 g) fennel seeds

1 tablespoon (6.5 g) coconut flour

1 pound (454 g) ground meat (beef and pork, or turkey and chicken)

1 egg

1 tablespoon (14 g) ghee, coconut oil, or other high-heat oil

1. In a large bowl, mix together the pesto, fennel seeds, coconut flour, ground meat, and egg until well blended.

2. Preheat a large skillet or shallow saucepan on medium heat, and melt the ghee in it.

3. Using an ice cream scoop or spoon, shape the meat mixture into balls and place them in the skillet, leaving space between the meatballs.

4. Brown the meatballs for about 5 minutes on each side.

5. At this point you can continue cooking the meatballs until they're cooked completely—about 10 minutes more—or add marinara sauce to the skillet and cover and simmer on a low heat for another 10 minutes.

6. Serve warm, with spaghetti squash or your favorite pasta, if desired. Store leftover meatballs covered in the refrigerator for a few days, or freeze for a few months.

Yield: About 10 meatballs

Tomato Chutney

•Gluten-Free   •Grain-Free   •Low-Sugar   •Dairy-Free
•Paleo   •Nut-Free

This chutney goes well with most savory breads and makes a great topping for the Garlic-Cauliflower Breadsticks (page 31). It's easy to make and tastes much like tomato sauce with concentrated flavors of roasted onion and pepper. Spread the chutney on any pizza dough, or use it as a dipping sauce.

1 pint (about 25) cherry tomatoes, sliced in half

1 red, yellow, or orange bell pepper, sliced into strips

1 small red onion, peeled and diced into small pieces

1 teaspoon (6 g) salt

1 tablespoon (6 g) honey or maple syrup

2 tablespoons (30 ml) olive oil

1. Preheat your oven to 350°F (175°C, or gas mark 4).

2. Place all the ingredients in a bowl and blend well.

3. Line a baking sheet with parchment paper and spread the tomato chutney mixture evenly across the paper.

4. Bake for 35 minutes, or until the edges begin to wrinkle a bit and brown.

5. Cool, then place the tomato mixture in a food processor or high-speed blender and pulse just a bit to blend but leave some chunks visible.

6. Serve warm or cool. Store in a sealed container in the refrigerator for up to a week.

Yield: 2 cups (300 g)

Roasted Cherry Tomatoes

•Gluten-Free   •Grain-Free   •Low-Sugar   •Dairy-Free
Option   •Paleo   •Nut-Free

Roasted cherry tomatoes are packed with flavor. I love using them in a variety of dishes, such as the Pesto Flatbread Pizza (page 35), and any dish that needs a pop of flavor. They're especially great as a substitute for tomato sauce.

1 pint (about 25) cherry tomatoes, halved

¼ cup (60 ml) olive oil

1 tablespoon (20 g) maple syrup, honey, or balsamic vinegar

¼ teaspoon salt

1. Preheat your oven to 350°F (180°C, or gas mark 4).

2. Place all the ingredients in a bowl and blend with a spoon.

3. Line a baking sheet with parchment paper or nonstick surface and pour the mixture onto the baking sheet.

4. Bake for 30 minutes.

5. Cool and use in a recipe or serve as a side with a meal. Store in a sealed container in the refrigerator for about a week or in the freezer for a few months.

Yield: About 1 cup (150 g)

Chicken Strips

•Gluten-Free   •Grain-Free   •Dairy-Free   •Low-Sugar   •Paleo   •Egg-Free Option

Chicken strips (also known as chicken fingers and chicken nuggets) are fun for lunch, dinner, or as a snack, and they're great to eat cold in a summer picnic lunch along with the honey mustard dip (see sidebar below).

To make this egg-free, eliminate the egg and dip the chicken directly in the flour mixture. Most of it will still stick to the chicken as it cooks in the oil as long as the oil and skillet are hot enough. Another option is to add about 1 teaspoon (7 g) of ground flaxseed to the flour mixture.

1½ pounds (680 g) chicken breast, sliced into strips

1 large egg

1 tablespoon (11 g) Dijon or stone-ground mustard

½ teaspoon salt

½ teaspoon cayenne pepper

½ teaspoon black pepper

¾ cup (72 g) blanched almond flour

¼ cup (26 g) coconut flour

2 tablespoons (28 ml) high-heat oil

1. Add the chicken, egg, and mustard to a bowl and blend well with a whisk or fork.

2. In a separate bowl add the salt, cayenne pepper, black pepper, almond flour, and coconut flour and blend well with a whisk or fork.

3. Spread the flour mixture across a plate. Place a paper towel (to absorb excess oil) on another plate to store the cooked chicken strips.

4. Heat a skillet or sauté pan over medium heat and add 2 tablespoons of cooking oil.

5. Remove each piece of chicken from the bowl, drip off the excess egg mixture, dredge lightly in the flour mixture, then add to the skillet. Brown the pieces for about 5 minutes on each side. Transfer to the prepared plate. Repeat until all the chicken strips are cooked.

6. Serve warm. Store in a sealed container in the refrigerator for a few days or in the freezer for a few months.

Yield: 3 to 4 servings

HONEY MUSTARD DIP

A very simple honey mustard dip!

¼ cup (80 g) honey

1 tablespoon (11 g) Dijon mustard or other mustard

Blend the honey and mustard together in a small bowl.

Yield: ¼ cup (80 g)

RESOURCES

Ingredients

Almond flour: Honeyville (www.honeyvillegrain.com), Tropical Traditions (www.tropicaltraditions.com), Edward & Sons (www.edwardandsons.com), Nuts.com (www.nuts.com), Digestive Wellness (www.digestivewellness.com), JK Gourmet (www.jkgourmet.ca)

Amazing Grass: Raw and reserve green superfood powder (www.amazinggrass.com)

Chocolate chips: Enjoy Life (www.enjoylifefoods.com)

Coconut flour: Honeyville (www.honeyvillegrain.com), Tropical Traditions (www.tropicaltraditions.com), Edward & Sons (www.edwardandsons.com), More Than Alive (www.morethanalive.com), Wilderness Family Naturals (www.wildernessfamilynaturals.com), Nuts.com (www.nuts.com), Digestive Wellness (www.digestivewellness.com)

Coconut milk: AROY-D (www.amazon.com), Natural Value (www.amazon.com); I prefer these brands because they have no additives and come in BPA-free containers.

Fire-roasted tomatoes: Muir Glen Organic Fire-Roasted Tomatoes with Chilies (www.muirglen.com)

Ghee: Pure Indian Foods (www.pureindianfoods.com), Purity Farms (www.purityfarms.com)

Gluten-free stone-ground cornmeal: Bob's Red Mill (www.bobsredmill.com)

Maple sugar: Shady Maple Farms (www.amazon.com), Coombs Family Farms (www.amazon.com)

Organic palm shortening: Spectrum Organics (www.spectrumorganics.com), Tropical Traditions (tropicaltraditions.com)

Unsweetened shredded coconut: Honeyville (www.honeyvillegrain.com), Tropical Traditions (www.tropicaltraditions.com), Edward & Sons (www.edwardandsons.com)

Whole cane sugar: Rapunzel (www.amazon.com)

Equipment

Springform pans: Kaiser Bakeware (www.kaiserbakeware.com)

Parchment paper: If You Care (www.ifyoucare.com), Beyond Gourmet (www.beyondgourmetcookingandbaking.com)

Loaf pans: Parish Magic Line (www.amazon.com)

Glass baking dishes with tops: Pyrex (www.pyrex.com)

Donut Maker: Sunbeam Mini (www.amazon.com)

Donut baking pan: Wilton (www.wilton.com)

Books

Amsterdam, Elana. *Gluten-Free Cupcakes: 50 Irresistible Recipes Made with Almond and Coconut Flour.* Berkeley, CA: Celestial Arts, 2011.

Fife, Bruce. *Cooking with Coconut Flour: A Delicious Low-Carb, Gluten-Free Alternative to Wheat.* Colorado Springs, CO: Piccadilly Books, 2011.

Walker, Danielle. *Against All Grain: Delectable Paleo Recipes to Eat Well & Feel Great.* Auberry, CA: Victory Belt Publishing, 2013.

ACKNOWLEDGMENTS

Writing a cookbook requires quite a large village, more like a sliver of the universe, which is what I experience (in a very good way!) when I post a recipe on Comfy Belly. There are so many people involved in the writing of a cookbook that I can't possibly do justice to this section, but I'll give it a try.

To my resident taste-testers, Sam, Max, and Craig, who let me know whether a recipe is thumbs-up or down, or what to change.

To my amazing extended family of recipe testers and Comfy Belly readers who welcomed these recipes into their homes and their bellies. I'm eternally grateful for your generosity, spirit, and honesty.

I sent out weekly recipes over a two-month period, and these adventurous people took the task and ran with it: Kim Ryder, Gary Charles, Caryn Schmitt, Sylvie Shirazi, Alexandra Enriquez, Daphne Whelahan, Chris Stephens, Rochelle James, Tacy Howell, Liana Masson, Sherry Kurtz, Erica Bulow, Shell Smith, Penny Whitman, Lucinda Henry, Michelle Law, Jessica Kettler, Venus Hayes, Katy Killiea, Katie Elliot, Amy Kauzloric, Janine Levenskunstenaar, Bethany Still, Alyson Fine, Rose Hegele, Lauren Garletts, Lisa Monnat, Lisa Durbin, Carolyn Curielli, Lisa Town, and Kathy Page.

To Amanda Waddell, for reaching out to me and providing insightful feedback and guidance along the way, and to the team at Fair Winds Press, thank you for getting this book in tip-top shape.

To Anne Depue for the guidance and support you lend to both the gritty and the fun part of writing a book.

ABOUT THE AUTHOR

Erica Kerwien is a writer, recipe developer, personal chef, and founder of Comfy Belly (www.comfybelly.com). She creates healthy recipes and treats for gluten-free, grain-free, dairy-free, and other lifestyles using simple, nutrient-dense ingredients. Her recipes are geared toward digestive health, weight management, and clean eating.

INDEX

P9-CME-449

PUBLIC LIBRARY

NOV 2 6 2017

RECEIVED

WITHDRAWN

"*The Healthy Coconut Flour Cookbook* is an amazing resource
for anyone who's interested in creating delicious and nutritious food."
—Robynne Chutkan, M.D., author of *Gutbliss* and founder of The Digestive Center for Women

♥ ♥ ♥

"This often underutilized flour is a fantastic way to add nutrients, fiber, and flavor to dishes,
especially for those looking for low-glycemic and grain-free options."
—Mary Purdy, M.S., R.D., www.nourishingbalance.com